AGENDA FOR AMERICAN JEWS

By ELI GINZBERG

Studies in the Economics of the Bible
The House of Adam Smith
The Illusion of Economic Stability
Report of American Jews on Overseas Relief, Palestine
    and Refugees in the United States
Grass on the Slag Heaps: The Story of the Welsh Miners
The Unemployed: I—Interpretation; II—Case Studies
The Labor Leader: An Exploratory Study
A Program for the Nursing Profession
A Pattern for Hospital Care
Agenda for American Jews
Occupational Choice: An Approach to a General Theory
    (With Others)
A Policy for Scientific and Professional Manpower
The Uneducated (With Douglas W. Bray)

AGENDA FOR
AMERICAN JEWS

by

ELI GINZBERG

KING'S CROWN PRESS

Columbia University   New York

KING'S CROWN PRESS is an imprint established by
Columbia University Press for the purpose of making
certain scholarly material available at minimum cost.
Toward that end, the publishers have used standardized
formats incorporating every reasonable economy that
does not interfere with legibility. The author has assumed complete responsibility for editorial style and for
proofreading.

PUBLISHED IN GREAT BRITAIN, CANADA, INDIA, AND PAKISTAN
BY GEOFFREY CUMBERLEGE, OXFORD UNIVERSITY PRESS,
LONDON, TORONTO, BOMBAY, AND KARACHI
MANUFACTURED IN THE UNITED STATES OF AMERICA

PREFACE

This book seeks to raise important questions, not to answer them. It is the privilege of every individual in a democracy to advocate a point of view and seek support for it. But it would be presumptuous for any one individual to propound answers to the host of complicated problems confronting American Jews. For the most part the answers must emerge from the thinking of the group itself.

This *Agenda* is the outgrowth of my belief that the social sciences can make an important, if limited, contribution to the effective solution of the complex problems that confront American Jews. Understanding is impossible and action blind unless complicated social situations can be simplified through analysis and evaluation. In this investigation I have relied upon the approach and methods of the social sciences, following the pattern of my earlier investigations devoted to analyzing significant aspects of group behavior.

The original idea for the investigation was provided by my friend, Mr. M. H. Blinken, President of the American Palestine Institute, who also furnished the resources required to carry it out. He had previously sponsored a significant research investigation into the economics of the Near East—*Palestine: Problem and Promise,* by Robert R. Nathan and others.

My father, Professor Louis Ginzberg, undertook to review with me the historical background and the contemporary implications of the several issues considered in this monograph. However, responsibility for the analysis and evaluation rests solely with me.

A small edition of this book was privately printed in the summer of 1949. In revising it for publication, I have benefited from the careful reading and suggestions of several colleagues and friends, particularly from that of Professor Moses Abramovitz of Stanford University and Dr. Sol W. Ginsburg, Vanderbilt Clinic, Columbia

University. My wife, Ruth Szold Ginzberg, aided me in the collection of materials and in the editing of the manuscript.

ELI GINZBERG

Columbia University
September 5, 1950

CONTENTS

INTRODUCTION

It is a striking characteristic of Americans to concentrate on activity and action at the expense of thought and evaluation. The problems engendered by conquering a continent were obvious; there was no need for the discoverers and exploiters of the wilderness to worry about philosophical subtleties—about where they were going and the alternative ways of reaching their goals. This basic characteristic of early American development has left a deep imprint upon all groups in the community as well as on the community at large.

Although many achievements of American life are the direct offspring of this deep-seated pragmatic emphasis on doing rather than reflecting, periodically evidence comes to the fore which indicates that this overemphasis, like all exaggerations, can be fraught with serious danger. To use a single illustration: Although the development of the atomic bomb is usually singled out as an example of American scientific genius, a more correct evaluation would emphasize that the basic theory was largely an European product while the American contribution was one of the engineering skills and economic resources.

The relative importance of action versus thought depends upon the nature of the problems which are awaiting solution. After a three- or four-year depression during which the accustomed remedies have failed to provide significant relief, there is little point to engaging in obfuscating economic debates for another three or four years: an experimental policy of constructive action is definitely preferable. At other times, when the pressures demanding a solution are less extreme, or when the choice among possible solutions is far from obvious, a reasonable investment in analysis and evaluation prior to action recommends itself.

This working paper has a twofold objective. It seeks to identify strategic problem areas with which American Jews are or should be concerned; and it further seeks to make explicit the boundaries within which solutions must be found.

[At present, American Jews are under considerable pressure. They must work out a policy with respect to the State of Israel. They must re-evaluate their relief and reconstruction programs now that the displaced persons problem is well on the way to solution and little if anything can be done to alter the fate of Jews living in Eastern Europe. All Jewry has been in a state of continuous crisis since the early 1930's and American Jews have of necessity concentrated on action programs during this period. But the time is overdue for them to assess their own development so that in the future they can make more constructive use of their potentialities and energies.

It is an axiom that no man, and no group of men, ever acts with respect to the present except in terms of some theory of the future, however unconscious they may be of this fact. We are likely to err when we are conscious of our goals and methods, and we are that much more likely to err if we proceed without conscious goals.

To contend that American Jews cannot escape the necessity of working out new solutions to new problems does not imply, of course, a belief that satisfactory and lasting solutions can be excogitated by theoreticians alone. The situations are too dynamic to permit anyone to foresee all the problems which are likely to arise. At most, a few which are already on the horizon can be used as bench marks. Every proposed solution should be tentative and subject to change. But the fact that the future is shrouded in uncertainty is no reason to avoid the onerous task of trying to evaluate such portents and clues as are available.

The burden of the following analysis is to delineate and assess the important forces that have given rise to the problems awaiting solution. The dichotomy between thought and action so largely characteristic of American development begins to dissolve. Analysis and evaluation are seen to be essential for policy determination. Since the conditions of life are forcing American Jews to resolve a host of difficult problems, a sharper delineation of the forces at work and a critique of the alternative solutions appear desirable.

I: JEWS AND JUDAISM

1. The evaluation of a complex social situation must always be selective. Theoretically it would be desirable to survey all aspects, but such an ambitious program is foredoomed to failure. The time required to gain control over the multiple variables at work in a concrete situation is so long that before all the factors have been brought under control the situation has changed and new factors have emerged. Hence every analyst must recognize from the outset the inherent limitations of his project and must reconcile himself to a selective rather than a comprehensive evaluation.

2. One reason for the deep-seated disagreement about current Jewish problems arises out of the fact that every analyst considers himself as competent as, if not more competent than, every other to select and appraise the strategic factors. The same individual who would not presume to treat a cold or the grippe is not hesitant to diagnose a complex historical situation or to prescribe a specific program for group action. Every protagonist is his own philosopher. He concerns himself with the problem because he feels deeply about it. Consequently, he seeks support for his emotional predilections.

3. Since the resolution of different points of view takes place in the public arena and since there is a close bond between analysis and action, each participant is concerned with the "propagandistic" implications of his position. He is more the politician than the philosopher for he must convince others if his values are to triumph.

4. Although each participant has "something to sell", it may be possible to distinguish among them according to the extent to which each feels obligated to deal with the important objective factors even when they fail to strengthen his case; according to whether he emphasizes the common ground between himself and his opponents or whether he emphasizes the differences and seeks to capitalize on the disagreements.

5. The desirability of stressing points of agreement rather than points of disagreement, of solidifying rather than splintering the community, is not self-evident. In matters of value, the attitude and behavior of the majority can never be solely determining. All significant change in social life is the result of the work of a believing minority which finally convinces an unbelieving majority of the wisdom of a particular approach. The single illustration of modern Zionism should suffice.

6. Although it is true that for many decades Zionist activity was a minority undertaking, the success of modern Zionism cannot be explained solely by the majority's finally accepting the preferred values of an aggressive minority. In two major respects, Zionist leadership relied on "objective facts"—the deep-seated feeling for Zion which pervaded the Jewish masses and the virulence of anti-Semitism in Europe.

7. Every individual who concerns himself with Jewish problems will formulate his answers in terms of his own value schemes. He will see the future of the group in light of his own aspirations and desires. This is true for all political and cultural activity, for all peoples; it is not an exclusive characteristic of Jews. However, the implications of this approach should be assessed against the unique background of Jewish development:

A. As a minority, Diaspora Jewry has always been under pressure from dominant forces in the Gentile environment and its own development cannot be understood except in relationship to these external pressures.

B. However, basic continuity was achieved by Diaspora Jewry because of the primacy of its own tradition and its scale of values.

C. As long as all Jews recognized the authority of tradition, the process of adjustment was buttressed by powerful principles which guided the selection of factors to be incorporated from the outside world as well as those to be rejected.

D. At present American Jews are divided between a majority who do not recognize the binding power of tradition, and a minority who continue to do so. Since matters of religious belief are not generally subject to deliberate compromise, it is difficult indeed for the religious minority in the United States to take cognizance of the "objective facts" in American Jewry.

8. Although it is inevitable that Jews with differing religious beliefs—or no beliefs at all—will read the future in light of their personal value schemes, and will seek to influence it accordingly, external conditions over which they have no control will frequently have the determining voice. Every objective person must admit that the catastrophic and constructive developments of the last two decades—the destruction of six million European Jews and the establishment of the State of Israel—were more a reflection of Hitler than of Jewish ideology.

9. Now that these two portentous events have occurred, the entire history of Jewry in Palestine and in the Diaspora will be markedly affected. Events of such magnitude are never isolated or peripheral; they are of the essence of the case. Just as they could not have been foretold, so no one can be sure of their influence and impact on the future. All that we know is that their impact is certain to be very great.

10. Despite the obvious need to be modest about our ability to read the future, it does not follow that because the unexpected and the exceptional does occur from time to time we are absolved from trying to assess the implications of present trends. Even the catastrophe in Europe and the success in Palestine cannot be divorced from the thinking and actions of earlier decades. Once Hitler marched into Poland there was no escape for Polish Jewry. But it is well to recall that during the 1920's and the early 1930's emigration from Europe was still possible. However, prevailing ideologies looked to eventual Jewish adjustment in Poland, not overseas, and, therefore, only a small number availed themselves of the oppor-

tunity to leave. Likewise, the birth of Israel would have been impossible but for the successful exploitation of opportunities by Palestinian Jewry aided by the liberality and political support of American Jews.

11. Jewish tradition has little sympathy either with the Christian doctrine of predestination in which man is saved or doomed at birth or with modern theories of determinism which maintain that the course of human events is controlled by the inevitable conflict of ideas or interest groups. The Jews have been told by their prophets and teachers that although they are the elected of God, their destiny is in their own hands. Not by belief nor prayer alone, but by their behavior will they be judged.

12.   The discussion up to this point can be recapitulated as follows:

A. Every evaluation of complicated social problems must be selective.

B. Selection will always be guided by the value scheme of the analyst—by his hopes and aspirations. It is because he feels strongly about certain values that he concerns himself with the problem.

C. Although it is essential in appraising a social problem to come to terms with the "objective facts", it is important to remember that one such objective fact is that the value schemes of the majority do change, particularly in response to successful propagandizing by a minority.

D. Despite the complications introduced by varying value schemes, significant trends may be ferreted out by searching for areas of agreement rather than by emphasizing divergences.

E. There are limitations inherent in analysis especially when it serves as a basis for forecasting. No one could have foretold recent developments in Jewish history.

F. Despite these limitations, the analyst has no alternative but to consider clearly and objectively the problems at hand, and to allow for future adjustments in his proposed solutions.

13. The following additional factors must be considered in appraising the current situation:

A. Even allowing for the manifold differences which exist between individuals and groups, it is reasonable to postulate that American Jews hold many values in common and further, that it would be useful to identify these common values.

B. It would furthermore be constructive to bring together individuals who share these values for the purpose of assessing the basic trends and institutions in American Jewish life.

C. The destruction of the larger part of European Jewry and the rebirth of Israel have precipitated a host of new problems for which American Jews, irrespective of ideological differences, must develop new approaches.

D. Since all Jewry, especially Diaspora Jewry, is particularly responsive to trends in the Gentile world, a periodic reassessment of important external forces is essential.

14. This particular approach is predicated upon the following:

A. Although marked variations in basic values can be found to exist among various sectors of American Jewry, the trend is definitely in the direction of a narrowing, rather than a broadening of these differences. The marked diminution in the number of new immigrants during the last thirty-five years has greatly reduced the previous religious, educational, social and economic variability. Moreover, there is every likelihood that this trend will continue.

B. Increasingly, the value schemes of many Jews can no longer be differentiated from other groups in the community.

C. In the past, communal agreement was achieved mainly in the area of fund-raising, because all sectors of American Jewry wanted to share in the support of the needy. Major efforts were devoted to raising larger and larger sums.

D. Since American Jewry represents a voluntary community in which no effective religious or legal sanctions exist to force the individual to discharge his communal responsibilities, the long-standing neglect of thought in favor of action has led to marked atrophy in the intellectual and cultural life of American Jews, at least with respect to their Judaism. The activists long ago usurped positions of prominence, and forced those whose contributions lay in the realm of ideas into the background.

15. These trends have serious implications because:

A. Jewish tradition does not permit the individual Jew to discharge his personal obligations to the community merely by making liberal donations to charity and by following the dictates of a professional leadership.

B. Professionalism presents a particular danger to a community which by its very essence is voluntary. It tends to reduce the number of active participants to a very few, and those few are not likely to be imaginative and constructive.

C. Professionalism presents a further danger because it facilitates the concentration of power in a few leaders and frequently turns issues of policy into struggles for organizational control and dominance.

D. The development of professionalism is particularly unfortunate at this stage of Jewish history because American Jewry has reached a relatively higher level of general education than any Jewry in history; hence American Jews might be expected to participate more actively and intelligently in communal undertakings.

E. The success of the professionals must in large part be explained by the marked ignorance of most American Jews in matters of Jewish interest and import. A sensible man, especially if he is preoccupied, as so many American Jews are, with earning a living, tends to simplify his life by looking to the leadership in areas where he does not consider himself competent.

F. A large and increasing number of American Jews would probably like to participate in Jewish affairs on a more meaningful level than that of fund-raising. But the present structure of the community affords them few opportunities.

II: TRENDS IN JEWISH LIFE

1. American Jews can be divided into three major groups with respect to the intensity of their relations to Judaism:

A. The leadership and the bureaucracy who devote the major portion of their time to the furtherance of Jewish causes, and those religious or secular Jews to whom one or another aspect of Judaism is so compelling that one can say that Judaism is their basic "avocation".

B. The moderately interested—the moderately participating member of the community who invests a considerable portion of his emotional energy, time, and financial resources in the support of Jewish institutions but whose major anchorage is in other fields.

C. The individual whose connection with Jewish activity is nonexistent or extremely limited; who may go to religious services on the High Holy Days and who may contribute to Jewish charities, but who has no deep emotional attachment to Judaism.

2. The following important subgroups can be distinguished:

A. There are many Jewish workers, especially in the large urban centers, who live in a world peopled almost exclusively by Jews. These workers live in Jewish neighborhoods; their employers are Jews; their co-workers are Jews; and their social life is limited almost exclusively to fellow Jews. However, despite the intensity of their exposure to things Jewish a large percentage of these workers have little direct involvement in Jewish life—synagogal, communal, Zionistic. Although they are Jews, they have no vital relation to Judaism. To a lesser degree, this applies to certain members of the middle class who likewise live in a Jewish environment without adopting a positive attitude towards it.

B. The escapist who, without being willing to go as far as conversion, deliberately reduces to the irreducible minimum his connections with fellow Jews and Jewish institutions. Numerically these escapists are relatively unimportant, but it should be remembered that their members frequently include individuals of considerable economic power and intellectual competence.

C. Although American Jewry is primarily urban, in fact predominantly metropolitan, there are many Jews who live in small towns and rural communities throughout the United States. Irrespective of their interests and values, these isolated Jews are usually unable to support such basic institutions as synagogues, Hebrew schools, community centers; and they are frequently located considerable distances from larger Jewish communities. Their ties with Judaism are thus loosened, although not necessarily by desire.

3. The foregoing attempt to distinguish among Jews in terms of the intensity of their relations to Judaism proceeded in formal terms; the principal criterion was the investment of a man's time and energy in Jewish activities. Yet we must realize that in all matters affecting values consideration must be given not only to the overt behavior but also to basic motivation. If one seeks to broaden the category scheme to take cognizance of motives, the following observations are relevant, especially in evaluating the leadership:

A. There are a considerable number of "Jewish leaders" who, although they contribute of their money, time, and energy to the furtherance of particular Jewish causes, frequently most liberally, nevertheless seem to be negatively oriented to Jewish values. Their outstanding characteristic is a basic "uneasiness" about their identification with the Jewish community. One cannot gainsay the impression that they are in Jewish work largely because they have been unable to find satisfactory alternatives. Whatever their unconscious motivation may be, devotion to the ideals of Judaism does not seem to be determining.

B. Another type of leadership is typified by an excessive aggressiveness and positivism about particular Jewish causes. The fact that these demagogic leaders are usually identified with a single Jewish undertaking rather than with the broad gamut of Jewish work is an *a priori* basis for suspecting that their very intensity is enmeshed in their own power drives. The frequent irascibility of their actions must place them under suspicion, for they seem unable to differentiate the security of their own leadership from the values of the cause which they lead.

4. Important aspects of contemporary Jewish life in America (see Chapters IV through VII) become more easily comprehensible when they are considered against the background of three major trends:

A. Too little weight has been ascribed to the collapse of the religious foundation of contemporary Judaism. Starting in the early part of the nineteenth century and rapidly gaining momentum, the belief in revelation—the basic foundation of Western religion—became undermined. The full impact of this radical change is difficult to assess because it represents a phenomenon unique in Western civilization. This is a new development and has not yet run its full course. As far as American Jewry is concerned, the following observations on this changed role of religion should be considered:

a. Although a forecast of the future religious orientation of American Jews would be venturesome, there is little basis for assuming any reversal of the present trend. It is impossible to contemplate a large-scale revival of orthodoxy in which the majority of American Jews would again recognize the overriding authority of the Bible and tradition. The counter-assumption of a continuing thinning of the ranks of the orthodox is the more plausible, in view of contemporary trends in immigration, education, and general culture.

b. Despite this current and probable future trend away from orthodoxy, it is important to note that the major alternative—Reform Judaism—has not shown real strength, and that its ability to hold its ground in recent years is a result of its re-emphasis on major aspects of Jewish tradition, including Zionism.

c. With the religious foundations of Judaism greatly weakened, the synagogue—the basic institution of Diaspora Jewry—has been directly affected. And the manifold attempts of the synagogue to reinforce itself through expansion into new realms—social activities, adult education, contemporary affairs, the arts—have not been too successful. The rabbis judge their own strength and success by the numbers who attend their lectures and the size of the contributions which they are able to elicit from their members, not by their ability to provide that spiritual leadership which should be reflected in the daily lives of their congregants.

d. Although orthodoxy has been losing ground constantly, a considerable number of American Jews still retain membership in synagogues which officially adhere to tradition. Even if the members fail to observe religious law and customs in their daily lives, their leaders are committed to upholding tradition.

B. Closely associated with the weakening of the religious core has been the almost total disregard of Jewish law, which in the past was both the major defense against assimilation and the major creative force for adjustment. Two important consequences of this greatly weakened position of the law are:

a. The present greatly diminished power of the authority of tradition will further decline, so that in time only a few American Jews will recognize the sanction of Jewish law even in the area of marriage, divorce, and related problems, the last outpost of rabbinical authority at the present time.

b. The gap between current practice and the tradition of Sabbath observance and dietary laws is so wide that a real danger exists that these institutions will soon lose the last vestige of meaning for the majority. It is not possible for the Sabbath and dietary laws to play a constructive part in American Jewish life so long as the breach between legal theory and actual practice is as great as at present. Yet if a small minority continues to adhere to the older forms because of strong religious conviction, it will be exceedingly difficult, if not impossible, to secure general assent to the establishment of new norms more in keeping with existing practice.

C. Not only is the American Jewish community forced to operate without the major support of the sanction of religious and legal tenets, it is also forced to manage without governmental status, which, as in the case of most European countries, enabled the Jewish communities to levy taxes and thereby facilitated the carrying out of communal programs.

5. In the entire history of the Diaspora no group of Jews has even been confronted with a problem comparable to that facing American Jewry, namely to organize and operate a community without internal sanctions (religion and law) and without external sanctions (recognition by the state). The unique aspects of this situation can be outlined as follows:

A. The ability of Jews to act jointly depends first and last on the emergence of a set of values that will be accepted voluntarily by large numbers who in turn will discipline themselves to make sacrifices for the support of these values.

B. Recently, a force of very considerable strength which is tending to weld many American Jews together is their fight against various types of anti-Semitic onslaughts ranging from social exclusion and economic discrimination to physical assault.

C. Forced to structure itself without the help of formal sanctions, it is not surprising that the Jewish community, if one can talk of a community at all, is loosely integrated. Inevitably a high degree of competition exists among the various Jewish organizations, each one of which can survive and grow only as it is able to convince potential supporters that it can further particular values in which they are, or should be interested. Although competition is considerable, many organizations of questionable value and efficiency manage to survive because of the liberality of the community which is frequently undiscriminating because it lacks specialized knowledge requisite for mature judgment.

6. So far we have noted that American-Jews can be subdivided into three major groups:

A. Those who are intensely concerned with Jewish problems.

B. The moderately interested group.

C. The peripheral group.

And we have further noted that Jews in the United States live in an environment typified by the following:

D. A greatly weakened religious foundation.

E. A substantial disregard of Jewish law.

F. The absence of formal governmental status.

7. The foregoing suggests that lack of emphasis on religious values has led to the partial eclipse of the synagogue as the dominant institution in Jewish life. With minor exceptions, this weakened position of the synagogue has placed the rabbinate on the defensive:

A. The rabbis have tended to "cater" to their congregants by offering them every value but religious values.

B. Out of personal frustration many rabbis have sought for greener pastures and have found their satisfaction in the leadership of political and charitable enterprises.

C. This reorientation of the rabbinate has led to a de-emphasis on scholarship, formerly the hallmark of the religious leader.

D. The principle of the vicious circle has been operating. The weakened position of the synagogue has made it impossible for the theological seminaries to attract many superior young men; and the resulting weakness of the rabbinate has made it difficult to reverse the trend away from the synagogue. An able rabbi can, however, contribute materially to raising the fallen prestige of the synagogue—at least in terms of current criteria such as size of membership, a fine edifice, manifold communal activities.

8. The weakening of religious faith is largely responsible for the substantial disregard of Jewish law. Reform Judaism challenged the law in its entirety and greatly accelerated the disregard of all tradition. Even though Reform Judaism has been unable to attract into its fold the majority of American Jews, it has nonetheless provided a powerful rationale for nonobservance. Pressed by the realities of life—the need to earn a living which usually entailed working on the Sabbath, the extreme difficulties of observing the dietary laws out of the home, and, perhaps most important, the uncongenial nature of orthodoxy in the American environment—large numbers of American Jews who did not join the Reform movement nevertheless threw off the burden of the law. Each man became an authority unto himself with the result that there exists today the most amazing galaxy of adjustments in which people observe one or another aspect of the dietary laws. In times of personal crisis many prefer the traditional ceremonials, but for the most part their life is a constant challenge to both the

spirit and the form of the law. Two further aspects bearing on the position of Jewish law in contemporary American life should be noted:

A. There has developed, especially among that large sector of American Jewry which is affiliated with conservative congregations, a marked dichotomy between the behavior of the vast majority of the congregants—which is largely non-observant—and the expected and required behavior of the rabbi. Although not without parallel in Jewish history, such a sharp disparity between the behavior of the congregation and its leader is basically unhealthy.

B. A particularly unpleasant influence of the general environment has found expression in the commercialism which has entered into the supervision of the production and marketing of goods and services prepared in accordance with ritual regulations. Although the ready acceptance of techniques that permeate American business is one explanation for the growth of this "religious commercialism", a second factor of importance has been the extreme financial vulnerability, particularly of immigrant orthodox rabbis who were unable to eke out a living by limiting their duties to the care of their congregants.

9. The weakening of religious values also exercised a significant influence on Jewish education which historically had been intertwined with religious observance. Only the educated man could be a religious man. As parents became estranged from the synagogue and from participation in group or familial ceremonials, they exerted less and less pressure on their offspring to acquire even the essentials of a Jewish education. Although many rabbis have tried to meet this threat by the establishment of Sunday Schools, the education of the young can be furthered only if parents are interested in preserving traditional values. But many parents are much more concerned about the social values of their class than about specifically Jewish values.

10. The marked weakness of the synagogue, which has been paralleled by the weakness of Jewish law and Jewish education, might lead one to believe that the community cannot be structured—for religion, law, and education are basic institutions. American Jews did, however, direct considerable energy into the creation of new communal forms, of which the most conspicuous have been: On the social level—lodges, community centers, etc.; for the care of the needy—federations, welfare funds, etc.; and on the ideological front—Zionist groups, defense committees, etc.

A. The fact that American Jews have created special organizations to provide for their leisure activities flows largely from the fact that the principal manifestation of anti-Semitism in the United States has been social. It is interesting to note that even American trade unions have been unable to challenge successfully the ethnic separatism in the social life of their members.

B. The marked degree of heterogeneity which long characterized American Jewry—largely a reflection of successive and continuing waves of immigrants from different parts of Europe—placed almost insuperable hurdles in the path of group action; for a long time, the only meeting ground was "charity". Irrespective of one's social or economic status, or political or religious beliefs, it was possible to join with others to raise funds for the Jewish needy at home and abroad. The outstanding success of Jewish philanthropic efforts in the United States, although in part a reflection of the generally higher level of charitable contributions of the New World as compared to the Old World, also reflects the fact that unity of effort among Jews could be achieved only in this area. Many of the ablest and most energetic Jewish leaders found it more satisfying to devote their energies to charitable causes because of the support and approval which they could secure from their fellow Jews,

than to struggle in the backwaters of education, culture, and
politics.

C. Until the advent of Hitler, except for those who held strong
religious convictions, only a small minority of American
Jews concerned itself with "ideological" questions. To the
extent that they did, they concentrated on "defense problems" that is, on fighting individuals and groups which
threatened their basic security. The only other significant
expression of ideological preoccupation was found on the
Zionist front, where a small but ardent group had long been
active. At one time the only issue of major importance on
which American Jews differed was in their support of
Zionism. But even this division had relevance more for the
leadership than for the large majority of followers. And
even this single difference gave way under the impact of
Hitler and World War II.

11. On the basis of the foregoing preliminary observations,
the following tentative characterization of the present structure
and functioning of the American Jewish community is ventured:

A. Despite the major crisis in Jewish life which has been with
us for the last twenty years it is probably true that the
majority—the vast majority of American Jews—feel little
compulsion to adopt a positive attitude (and behavior) to
Judaism. The criteria which are customarily employed to
measure intensity of Jewish orientation such as charitable
contributions, pressure group action on the political front,
etc., are grossly misleading.

B. The cornerstones on which Diaspora Judaism built its life—
religious belief and legal practice—no longer exist for the
vast majority of American Jewry. Since we have no example
in the long and diversified history of the Jews which would
point to the possibility of survival—a creative survival—
without these major supports, there is ground for deep concern.

C. The synagogue and the learned men attached to it have been supplanted in the United States by powerful secular institutions such as social centers, welfare funds, and political groups.

D. Cautious estimates would point to the conclusion that the number of active participants in Jewish life is very small. A disproportionate degree of responsibility and control—disproportionate for a group which relies on individual responsibility and participation—is in the hands of the leadership.

E. American Jews, leaders and followers alike, lack knowledge of their own history and tradition, an ignorance which inevitably places a major barrier in the way of their search for guides to current adjustment and growth.

F. A continuing, though undetermined, loss in effective manpower results from intermarriage which is probably more prevalent among the wealthy and talented members of the community.

III: COMMON GROUND

1. Because membership in the Jewish community is entirely voluntary, subject only to the social compulsions from within and without, Jewish values can survive in the United States only to the extent that they have the strength to keep old adherents and attract new ones.

2. No analysis of Jewish life in America can proceed very far without cognizance of the marked variation in the interests and active participation of American Jews in various phases of contemporary Judaism. These differences in interests and intensity are likely to continue.

3. The radical transformation which has occurred during the last century, particularly in the United States, has weakened the religious and legal foundations of Judaism. As a consequence of this cultural change social, charitable, and ideological organizations have not only multiplied but have been able to compete successfully with the synagogue which theretofore had been the focal center of Jewish life.

4. In light of the foregoing, this chapter will stress the need of searching for the common ground and will suggest the boundaries in which it must be sought.

5. Since few men can live without membership in a group and since the very essence of Judaism is a sense of identity with its past and future, the search for common ground in American Jewish life is not optional but mandatory. Since each subgroup will define its mission for itself, there exists a real danger that disagreements and struggles among the various subgroups will neutralize all effective action. Only by finding and broadening the common ground among the various subgroups can the total investment of time, energy, and money made by American Jews lead to constructive ends.

6. Every voluntary community is confronted with multiple difficulties. Its life is largely a composite of the lives of various subgroups. In the absence of overriding conditions, it is relatively easy for adherents of a particular point of view to become so involved with furthering their particular values that they ignore the implications of their actions on other values. Towards the values of other subgroups, they hold either a neutral or negativistic attitude, for in a very real sense every subgroup is a competitor of every other. Moreover, since a large part of the meaningfulness of affiliation comes from the shared experiences in organizational life— the meetings, the parties, the politics—the growth of a subgroup measured in' the conventional terms of size of membership and financial resources frequently obscures the lack of progress which is being made to further the basic values of the organization. Because the growth of an organization frequently becomes an end in itself; and because each subgroup competes with every other to gain adherents, one has a situation best described by Hobbes as "the war of one against all".

7. The only restraints against the extreme wastefulness of group competition which on occasion degenerates into a fight for survival, are external threats or internal controls. As far as external threats are concerned, nothing short of a major onslaught on the basic rights of all Jews—virulent anti-Semitism crystallized into a political movement—would be likely to lead to a voluntary limitation of action by particular subgroups. Even so dominant a threat as that provided by recent history will not lead to self-imposed restraints, usually because each group fears for its survival unless it can continue to operate as a separate and distinct entity, unless it can, in the language of the market place, "keep its trade-mark before the public". This explanation recognizes that there may well be serious difficulties standing in the way of effective compromise and joint action where major differences in ideology do in fact exist.

8. If subgroups will not be moved to limit their freedom as a result of external pressures, there remain only internal controls.

In a voluntary community without legal structure and without formal sanctions, the only restraint to independent action by individual subgroups is in a widescale adherence to common values. Individuals who share basic values will, when necessary, restrain themselves (and their particular subgroups) in order to further broad community objectives.

9. In an autocratic society, or even in a democratic society, methods exist for resolving conflict situations. Either the king and elders decide among the alternatives or the people at large are afforded an opportunity to vote on the different proposals before them. No such mechanism does exist, or in fact can exist, in a truly voluntary community since one group has no way of compelling other groups to support a common program. Since a voluntary community is, however, frequently confronted with the need for joint action and since it cannot rely on political or legal techniques to secure the required action, it must fall back on the only course which remains—the development of a common philosophy for its members.

10. Since we know from experience that despite great diversity, American Jews have been able to work co-operatively for the accomplishment of selected objectives—in particular, overseas relief and the upbuilding of Palestine—it is reasonable to presuppose that substantial common ground does exist among the members of the community. Because of the demonstrated importance of recognizing and broadening this common ground, careful analysis is required to assess the most favorable area for expansion.

11. No individual Jew can reach a tolerable personal adjustment, nor assuredly can any sizable group of Jews hope to deal intelligently with the problems that are constantly precipitated by the changing pattern of history unless they can orient themselves to the Jewish past—to the history of the Jewish people as written in its accomplishments, defeats, and never-ending trials. At present the level of Jewish literacy, not only of large numbers of American Jews, but unfortunately also of many leaders, is phenomenally low.

12. Although knowledge of the Jewish past is a major pre-requisite for the intelligent assessment of problems in the Jewish present, such knowledge alone is not a reliable guide. For instance, an intimate acquaintance with contemporary Jewries is necessary to insure that American Jews do not unwittingly jeopardize the welfare of a vulnerable Jewish group which is living in a hostile environment. The destruction of most of European Jewry has tragically simplified this particular problem. Nevertheless, American Jewry should be well informed about Diaspora communities in five sectors of the world:

A. Moslem countries.

B. Western Europe.

C. Eastern Europe.

D. Canada, South Africa, Australia.

E. South America.

13. In addition to the need for a broad knowledge of the Jewries of old, as well as of those contemporary communities which have managed to survive, American Jews have an obligation to be intimately acquainted with developments in Israel. Since the issuance of the Balfour Declaration the Palestine problem has played an increasingly significant part in the life of the Diaspora, especially in Europe, the United States, and South Africa. Long before the establishment of the Jewish State, the Palestine issue was exercising an increasingly important influence on the way in which American Jews approached the entire gamut of their problems. Now that the State has become a reality, and it is in a position to make a very large contribution to the development of Judaism, it is inevitable that its impact on the Diaspora will be very great. This does not deny that the Diaspora, and in particular American Jewry, may in turn exercise a considerable influence on developments in Israel.

14. Without considering at this time the means to accomplish the desired end, it is clear that every American Jew who desires to

play a part in the determination of his own future and the future
of American Jewry is duty-bound to be literate concerning:

A. The history of the Jews.

B. The position and problems of contemporary Jewries in other
parts of the world.

C. The developments in Israel which will doubtless exercise
an unique influence on the future of Judaism.

15. Implicit in this emphasis on history is the conviction that
the essence of being a Jew is a deep feeling of identity with the
Jews of the past, the present, and the future. It is recognized that
individuals will differ in their capacity to identify themselves with
other Jews. Some will feel the association very deeply, others much
more superficially; but every Jew must experience it to some degree.
Despite these marked differences which will largely determine the
intensity of each individual's Jewishness, the simple fact of identification, complete or partial, has significance for the behavior of
every Jewish group.

16. Because of the paramount role of tradition in Jewish life,
the obligation is imposed on every Jewish group, irrespective of
its particular program and orientation, to act with circumspection
and restraint whenever its actions are likely to bring it into conflict with tradition. It does not follow that each and every institution of the past must remain hallowed. The fact that the vast
majority of American Jews no longer feel bound by religion and
tradition underlines the inherent difficulty of the problem. The
group has denied its own tradition, yet this tradition has been the
source of its major strength. But it would be false to contend that
American Jewry has denied its tradition in its entirety. The forced
retreat of Reform Judaism to ceremonialism and Zionism is the best
proof of the partial continuity of tradition in American Jewish life.

17. During the last few decades the various components of
Jewish tradition have been sifted by the different groups—that is,
by all except the extreme orthodox for whom the problem does not

exist, since tradition per se is binding on them. The major subgroups in the community have been struggling, largely unsuccess-
fully, to select from among the great riches of tradition those
elements which can be woven into contemporary life. This difficult
undertaking has been handicapped by the fact that the conservative
rabbinate which might have been expected to assume leadership
was caught in the serious dilemma of not daring to satisfy the
liberal majority for fear of alienating the believing minority. In
this, as in many other respects, Israel may soon make a significant
contribution, for in Israel a sifting of tradition must be made. A
modern state cannot function within the limitations of Talmudic
precepts. Much will be discarded, but the remainder will be vitalized.

18. Although the basic trends in American Jewish life during
the first half of the twentieth century will be discernible only in
the years to come when time has provided the essential perspective,
it is probable that history will stress the philanthropic largess of
American Jews. Jewish communities throughout the entire world
were able to secure assistance in the United States—liberal assistance, and repeated assistance. This liberality of American Jews
should be appraised against the background that many givers had
little knowledge of, or feeling for, the beneficiaries; and many
others had a desire not to become too closely identified with their
brethren overseas. The third-generation Jew living in the Mid-
west had only the most tenuous ties with the struggling masses
in the Warsaw ghetto. And the socially elite Jews in the United
States patterned their lives so as to be more acceptable to their
Gentile neighbors, which meant that they sought to keep to a
minimum the bonds which tied them to other Jews of a lower
economic and social level. Yet both groups of American Jews have
been liberal in their support of charitable undertakings.

19. Even if we admit that financial largess did not itself be-
token a sense of cohesion with foreign Jewries; and even though we
recognize that many charitable American Jews have made studied
efforts to disassociate themselves from their fellow Jews, there is a
moral which runs through the story, particularly as it bears on the

group. Despite the inability of many individual Jews to resolve the problem of where to seek security and stability—within the Jewish group or outside of it—the behavior of the Jewish group as a whole has attested to its ability and willingness to follow tradition which holds that every Jewish community is the brother and guardian of every other. American Jews did not necessarily share many of the values of the Jewries whom they succored; nor did American Jews have much understanding and knowledge of the way of life of these foreign Jews. Yet the bond was there.

20. Although Jewish life must be deeply rooted in the past, since it derives its strength from the shared experiences in history, Judaism is always oriented to the future. Growth and survival are its major preoccupation. Despite the fact that one becomes a Jew by the actions of others—one's parents—one remains a Jew by his own actions. This is particularly true at a time like the present when the community is without sanctions and the affirmation of one's Jewishness is solely a matter of personal responsibility. It is true that the Jewish community receives assistance from the Gentile world which has set up barriers to easy assimilation. But many Jews who remain within the group maintain a substantially passive relationship to Jewish life, limiting their affirmation to occasional contributions to Jewish charity.

21. It is a reflection on the intellectual and emotional attitude of large numbers of American Jews that they are largely unaware of the implications of their passivity upon the development of their own lives, and particularly the lives of their children. Admittedly the problem of identification with the Jewish community is difficult, especially for parents who were brought up without the constructive support of tradition and a positive orientation to Jewish life. But though one can understand the nature of the difficulty, one must recognize that it can be resolved only by positive action. The more the individual can identify himself with the positive aspects of Judaism, the more likely he is to break through the impasse and find a way out. Among the major contributions of

Israel to Jewish life in America—a contribution which will doubt-less be vastly increased in the coming years—is the pull which it has been able to exert even on previously estranged Jews.

22. Essentially the adjustment of the individual and, more particularly, the group depends upon:

A. A feeling of continuity with the Jewish past.

B. A sense of identity with other Jewries.

C. An awareness that the future of Judaism in the United States requires a personal affirmation.

23. Because of its long and diversified experiences, every Jewish group is in need of a learned leadership. For in the absence of learning, action will inevitably be blind. Although one can look forward to a reasonably informed group of Jews in the United States, it would be too much to expect that everyone will acquire expert knowledge and skills, the requisites for intelligent decision making. The fact is, however, that leadership of the American Jewish community has been largely in the hands of wealthy laymen who, despite many admirable qualities, have been conspicuously ignorant of the history and traditions of their own people. Although men of means have always played an important role in Jewish leadership, in the past they were usually much better informed about Jewish culture and, moreover, they were forced to share their leadership with scholars and rabbis. With the weakening of the synagogue in America, the rabbis concentrated on developing their oratorical capacities and organizing ability, not on learning and scholarship. Hence, they too failed to develop scholarly competence.

24. The group usually secures the type of leadership it deserves. The cultural mediocrity of American Jewish leadership is largely a reflection of the unsettled stage of American Jewish life in which so large a part of the group has lacked background and knowledge. Moreover, the first efforts of the group, directed to organizing federations and welfare funds, community centers, and fraternal

orders, could proceed without making strenuous demands on the knowledge and culture of the leaders.

25. The fact that so large a proportion of American Jews have had at best only a moderate interest in Jewish affairs helps to explain why it has been relatively easy for many mediocre leaders to maintain themselves in power. Many Jews were pleased that certain individuals were willing to devote themselves to the management of Jewish activities. They were willing to support these leaders as long as the leaders did not make too many requests of them.

 26. Judaism holds each Jew personally responsible for the welfare of the group. Until a much larger number is willing to participate actively in Jewish life, which implies that they acquire a reasonable background of the facts and issues, and until they are willing to make a sizeable personal investment of time and effort, it is inevitable that a largely second-rate leadership will remain safely ensconced. The leadership, aware of its innate limitations, will instinctively manipulate the situation to remain in control rather than to work towards a larger and better informed participating group.

27. The overwhelming requirement of American Jews to increase their own literacy and to be led by competent and scholarly men and the present difficulties which stand in the way of achieving these essential and necessary reforms are not easily reconciled. However, there are several favorable elements in the situation.

A. American Jews have today reached the highest level of general education of any Jewry in the world. Increasingly American Jews are high school or college graduates. Even allowing for their lack of Jewish background, they should be increasingly sensitive to intellectual shallowness.

B. Since Jewish life can attract individuals only by the values which it can offer them; and since many will probably be drawn into Jewish activities in a search for intellectual and

moral clarity, such an influx should provide an opportunity
for constructive developments.

C. The major changes in the position of world Jewry brought
about by the holocaust in Europe and the establishment of
Israel will result in the obsolescence of many shallow
ideologies. Current events are forcing a radical re-evaluation.

28. For this process of re-evaluation in which the entire Jewish
community should participate, it is desirable to isolate significant
areas for concentrated appraisal. New approaches must be sought
in the area of:

A. The synagogue and the school.

B. Welfare activities.

C. Adjustment to Israel.

D. Relations to the Gentiles.

IV: SYNAGOGUE AND SCHOOL

1. Reference has previously been made to the unique role of the synagogue during the last two thousand years of Jewish life. The synagogue was the institution most responsible for structuring the life of the Jews who were without benefit of the normal supports of sovereignty and territory. No matter where Jews lived, whether on the banks of the Rhine or in the cities of Iraq, and no matter how greatly they modified their own traditions in response to local stimuli and pressures, there remained an integral core, the synagogue and its service, which was substantially the same in all communities.

The synagogue played an unique role in the history of the Diaspora. Judaism survived because the Jews were willing, if necessary, to sacrifice limb and life in order to maintain their beliefs and practices. Throughout these centuries religious conviction was not a matter of incidental importance—it was the essence of life itself.

3. It is important to remember that every adult male Jew was indissolubly bound to the synagogue, just as indissolubly as he was to the community. He had no options such as currently exist when a man can consider himself, and be considered, a Jew, even a good Jew, without assuming any formal obligation to the synagogue. The synagogue of old was not an independent institution. It was an integral part of the totality of religious life which encompassed almost every aspect of living. Many ceremonials were performed in the home; but a significant part of total religious observance was centered in and around the synagogue.

4. Although many have appreciated the fact that the synagogue long ago lost its strategic role they have not always interpreted this phenomenon correctly. During the last century and a half an increasing proportion of the population of Western Europe and America, Christian and Jewish alike, has experienced a major

revolution in its religious beliefs. The Biblical view of the world, the role of revelation, and the validity of basic tradition as expounded by the great religious teachers—have been seriously challenged. Large sectors of society no longer feel themselves bound by religious dogma and practice. Just as it is impossible to conceive of a Jew in the Middle Ages without his synagogue, so in turn it is very difficult to find a place for the synagogue in the life of a modern Jew to whom prayer, communal services, and ceremonialism have little meaning. The extent of the change can be demonstrated by the fact that while previously most Jews attended services three times daily, the majority today do not attend three times yearly.

4. Although the basic explanation for the weakened position of the synagogue is doubtless to be found in this religious revolution which has affected all of western civilization, there are a series of specific factors which have played a part in this radical transformation, particularly in the United States.

A. Daily attendance at the synagogue clearly involves difficulties for all except the most devout; and weekly attendance on the Sabbath has long been burdensome on individuals who must support themselves and their families. The conventional work week, until recently, has been six or a minimum of five and a half days. Most jobs have dictated that an employee must work on Saturday morning. It is no accident therefore that for many years the majority of the congregants in Conservative and Reform synagogues have been women and children.

B. Although many efforts were made to adapt the conventional service to the needs and desires of the congregants, a trend which led to the almost complete elimination of Hebrew prayers in Reform synagogues, the basic problem remained substantially intractable. The traditional service, if for no reason other than its venerability and universal acceptance, had a basic integrity. Deliberate and self-conscious changes of folk traditions are certain to be awkward and strained. There is almost a contradiction in terms in "modernizing" prayers whose power is largely an outgrowth of the collective genius of a people. But although the problem could not be resolved by sacrificing the old prayers, or by making use of them primarily in English translations, to follow the conventional order also had serious drawbacks. Since only a minority possess even a minimum knowledge of Hebrew, the traditional service can be meaningful to only a small number of the congregants. Although the Catholic Church has been able to structure its service so as to place primary responsibility for the mass on the priest, not on the congregants, such an approach is fundamentally alien to the synagogue in which there is no intermediary between the individual and the Divine. Unable to find the solution to this dilemma, the synagogue has inevitably been further weakened.

C. Long before the modern revolt against orthodoxy, individuals within the Jewish community from time to time had serious doubts concerning accepted dogmas and practices. However, unless they were willing to run the major risk of excommunication, they had little option but to put their doubts aside and turn their minds and energies into other directions. These skeptics had to submit to communal discipline and could buy their peace only through conformity. Today the situation is vastly different. It is definitely possible, and in fact has been for several generations, for an individual to participate actively and meaningfully in Jewish life without participating in any religious observance, on an individual or communal basis.

D. Although the main contribution of the synagogue of old was that it served as the focal center for religious observances, it supported other important values. Just as in medieval times the cathedral, through the beauty of its service, afforded the Christian masses an escape from the drudgery and barrenness of life, so the synagogue, by means of its adult educational mission, helped to enrich the lives of the Jewish group. The Sabbath and the holidays were days of rest; they were days of communal celebration; they were days on which the poor as well as the rich could share in the glories and riches of the past. And since there was no other place to which a Jew could go, and no other activity that he could enjoy on a Saturday morning, the synagogue was the principal "leisure-time" institution of Ghetto Jewry. Today the synagogue has a host of major competitors. It no longer possesses the monopolistic advantages of old.

E. The problem of Jewish adjustment has always been twofold—the adjustment of the Jews to their own tradition and their adjustment to the traditions and practices of the community in which they live. It is relevant that a large part of the Christian population of the United States—a very large part—does not attend church. This fact has doubtless exercised a significant influence on many Jews, obviously not on the orthodox nor the agnostic, but on the large middle group which is still searching to find itself.

F. A particular phenomenon in American urban development which has had a considerably weakening influence on the synagogue is the excessive mobility of the population. Frequent shifts in residence have contributed to the difficulties of developing firm ties between a family and a particular congregation. This problem has been less acute in the case of Reform temples whose members are permitted to ride to services. But location is a major obstacle for Orthodox and Conservative congregations where the law prohibits and custom looks askance at the use of private or public transportation on the Sabbath and holidays.

G. Closely associated with this influence of mobility on the position of the synagogue in American Jewish life is the definite class structure of many congregations. Historically, the synagogue was a place of worship for all—rich and poor, educated and uneducated. Because most synagogues in the United States are neighborhood institutions rather than community institutions and because neighborhoods tend to differ sharply from each other on the basis of average family income, radical class differences can be found to exist among many congregations. Since income is usually correlated with the length of time a family has been in America and therefore with the family's source of origin (the Jews of fourth- and fifth-generation American background are mostly of German extraction) there is an even larger gap between one congregation and the next, because the economic differentiating factors are reinforced by social and cultural forces. One significant implication of this class structure of American synagogues is the fear that many have that they will feel out of place or—worse still, will not be accepted if they seek to join the synagogue of their choice.

6. These further trends in synagogical life can be identified:

A. Despite the admitted decline in orthodoxy, it would be an error to conclude that all the non-orthodox are non-religious and have no need for or interest in congregational affiliation. Many people find satisfaction and solace in communal devotions; and there is probably a still larger number who might if some of the difficulties blocking their participation were removed. The shorter working week points to the elimination of one important barrier. Attendance at synagogue on Saturday mornings no longer means serious economic loss. The trend toward community, rather than neighborhood synagogues, especially noticeable outside of metropolitan centers, will help to remove the class barriers which in the past have stood in the way of many who desired to join.

B. Although Jewish law adopted a much more liberal and considerate policy with respect to women than did the legal systems of the other peoples of antiquity, women have played at most a minor role in the organized religious life of Jewry. Moreover, this role has been restricted to the home. In addition to the religious revolution of this past century, we have been in the midst of a "feminine" revolution, which has already resulted in tremendous changes in the role of women and which has by no means yet spent its strength. Some minor concessions have already been made to this revolution, even by groups who live by tradition, concessions which broaden the scope for women to participate in the religious life of contemporary Jewry. The outstanding development has been the institutionalizing of a confirmation ceremony for girls. But major adjustments must still be made if the synagogue is to attract women who comprise such an important source of potential strength.

C. We have noted that it is not only possible, but customary, for many persons without synagogical affiliation to play an active role in Jewish life, but this pattern is typical primarily in large metropolitan areas. In moderate-sized communities pressure is exerted not only on the potential leader, but on all who seek to identify themselves with the Jewish community, to join a synagogue. It is likely that with the reduction in immigration and with the other forces tending to make the Jewish community more homogeneous, pressures on individuals to join will increase and will prove effective.

D. Formal affiliation is important, but Judaism implies active participation. This in turn revolves around the question of whether the individual member and his family can find meaningful values in the synagogue. As far as the basic service is concerned, there will be no easy resolution of the difficulties involved in making it possible for Jews with little or no knowledge of Hebrew to appreciate the traditional service, while radical changes in this service would prove—if the experience of the Reform Movement is indicative—of little avail. But the middle ground is being explored with some success. A major key to the out doubtlessly the future of Jewish education.

7. There is a sound historic basis for discussing Jewish education in intimate relation to religion and the synagogue. Until recently they have been strands of the same fabric. Since one could not say his prayers and otherwise discharge his religious responsibilities unless he were able to read, basic education was a *sine qua non* for the religious man. For almost two thousand years Jewish communities have considered their primary schools the most important bulwark of Judaism. The community, having defined a minimum level of education as essential for all members, had to insure that this minimum was available not only for the rich who were able to pay for it but, more particularly, for the poor whose education had to be subsidized. Although great stress was laid on literacy, the Jews were not solely concerned with primary education. In the more advanced grades, demonstrated competence was the principal requirement for admission; the educational system became more selective and exclusive and reached an apex in the academy which was the training ground of the scholar. The Jews, like the Chinese, used their higher educational system as a training and testing ground for future leaders. Superior scholarship was the one certain road to the top.

8. Because of the close ties between education and religion, and because of the relatively minor role reserved for women in the organized structure of religious life, the educational system concentrated on boys. Since even the Reform movement has done little to alter significantly the role of the Jewish woman, Jewish education continues to be preoccupied with the training of males, although it is becoming increasingly responsive to the needs and desires of the female population.

9. No proper appraisal of Jewish education in the United States is possible unless one considers it in contrast with the structure which prevailed in Eastern Europe during the past centuries. Except for a few members of the upper classes and for a minority of

"free thinkers", Jewish education in Eastern Europe was special education. The Jewish child acquired a basic knowledge of Hebrew—though not usually fluency in the spoken tongue—an uneven acquaintance with the Bible, and, depending on how long he remained in school, a greater or lesser knowledge of the Talmud and other rabbinic literature. He knew literally nothing of Western culture, history, mathematics, or science. His was in fact an extremely specialized fare.

10. In the United States, the laws of the several states require that every child must receive instruction in the basic curriculum, either in public schools or in approved private schools; Jewish education becomes, by legal dictate as well as custom, complementary to secular learning. For most children the school day passes in a public institution in which there is no place for specialized courses in religion or culture. If parents want their children to acquire a broader background, the burden is on them to provide it. The only major alternative—and a very expensive one—is the establishment of a system, of parochial schools in which the religious and the secular subjects are taught in an integrated curriculum. A system of Jewish education which is forced to be complementary is by that very fact severely handicapped. It must compete with all other leisure-time activities—sports, music, recreation. The problem is further complicated because the children of the Protestant majority are largely free from these additional educational "burdens" which simply adds to the resistance of the average Jewish youngster when he is pressed to allocate time to Jewish studies.

11. Although the resistance on the part of the youngsters cannot be overlooked in any realistic appraisal of the situation, the major impediment may in fact be parental. By and large, children do not determine the distribution of their own leisure-time activities. To a large degree these are under parental control. The situation with respect to Jewish education can be epitomized in these terms: For the large number of parents who have at best only a moderate interest in Jewish values there is little incentive

to place Jewish education high on the list of leisure-time activities for their children; piano lessons, sports, and other activities take precedence.

12. One compromise which has found considerable favor, especially among the members of Reform congregations and to a lesser extent among others is, to limit the Jewish education of their children to participation in "Sunday School". For a long time when the Reform movement was anti-Zionistic and anti-traditional, education in Sunday School was circumscribed to a minimum of instruction in the stories of the Bible. In recent decades the curriculum has become somewhat more substantial and has included a more sympathetic understanding of Zionism and important Jewish institutions and ceremonials.

13. Parents who are more respectful of tradition have usually exerted greater pressure on their offspring, especially on their sons. They have tried to expose them to a broader type of Jewish education by sending them to a "Hebrew school" which meets three to five times a week for several hours per day. To acquire the essential knowledge for the Bar Mitzvoh ceremony was a major objective for every boy. Perhaps the overemphasis on this particular goal helps to explain the radical diminution in attendance after boys reach their thirteenth year.

14. Jewish education in the United States has been particularly handicapped by the following:

A. It is only within recent times that synagogues have increasingly assumed responsibility for the development of "Hebrew schools," although the "Sunday School" has from its inception been a congregational enterprise. In the absence of adequate planning and coordination on a community basis, there are limitations to the development of a large number of relatively small synagogical schools, but there are obvious advantages to using the organizational strength of the stronger congregations for the purpose of expanding Jewish educational facilities.

B. Since most welfare funds and federations from the start were assiduous in avoiding entanglements in ideological conflicts, they concentrated on "uncharged" areas such as the support of the needy, health, and social services. For a long time, they have been reluctant to assume responsibility for the partial or complete support of Jewish education. However, a marked trend in this direction is now discernible.

C. There is practically no educational system which can be self-supporting—which can rely exclusively upon income from tuition. Jewish education is no exception. Since many parents have been unable to meet even modest charges, and since it has not been feasible to have the paying pupils balance the budget, there has long been a need for voluntary contributions.

D. Because of the substantial disinterest in educational matters manifested by welfare funds and federations, special organizations have been established in many communities for the particular purpose of furthering Jewish education. These Boards of Jewish Education have been interested not only in securing funds to pay for the tuition of the poor but have also concerned themselves with more general problems— the training of teachers, professional salaries, curriculum, and allied matters. Although they have made considerable headway, they have been forced to struggle against a widespread apathy growing out of the lack of active interest on the part of most American Jews in a creative Judaism.

15. It is likely that some of the difficulties which have confronted Jewish education in the United States during the past decades will slowly be resolved as communities reassess the dangers of remaining aloof from the support of cultural objectives. Nevertheless, the major problems will not be easily resolved, as the following considerations emphasize:

A. The demands on time and the competition to use it for other purposes remain basic. The assumption that young American Jews will devote almost the whole of their leisure time to Hebrew education is obviously unrealistic. If the number of hours per week is brought within a tolerable level (for instance, seven) and if the quality of instruction is raised substantially above present standards, it may be possible to lengthen the number of years that children attend school. At the present time, the low level of efficiency of the educational process is demonstrated by the very high drop-out rate.

B. Recognizing the inevitable limitations of time, the amount of investment necessary to acquire minimum control over the Hebrew language warrants concern. If the secular high schools and colleges are used as a measuring rod, it is clear that most Americans find it exceptionally difficult to learn a foreign language, irrespective of how long they are exposed to formal instruction. Perhaps it will be possible in Hebrew schools to distinguish the linguistically gifted from the ungifted and spare the latter from an inordinate waste of time.

C. Education in the true sense of the word can never be limited and confined to a particular time and place. Obviously, there must be mutual support among the Jewish school, the synagogue, and the home if the school is to make headway. However, the synagogue will in turn depend for its vitality on the literacy of the congregants. And neither the synagogue nor the school will make much headway unless Jews become more interested in the furtherance of these forces in their daily lives. There are signs, however, that the low point in cultural indifference was reached and passed some time ago and that we are currently at the beginning of an upward spiral.

V: WELFARE

1. The support of its own poor and needy has long been one of the major objectives of all Jewish communities. The leaders of old repeatedly emphasized that it was the responsibility of the prosperous to care for the less fortunate. The fact that they returned to this theme time and again suggests that the wealthy were not eager to assume this responsibility. But after the destruction of the Temple and the dispersion of the Jews among the Gentiles, what had previously been a religious and ethical imperative became an economic and political necessity. A small and strange minority could survive amidst an aggressive and hostile majority only by developing a strong internal cohesion which would make it largely independent of the whims and wishes of the majority. Because of the pressures exerted by the alien environment, the Jews developed a group of educational and welfare institutions which were established and maintained entirely by the efforts of their own members.

2. Although the specific pattern differed from country to country and from century to century, the ability of Diaspora Jewry to create and support an elaborate group of social services was grounded in the right of self-taxation, a right which almost every Jewish community possessed.

3. The separation of church and state in the United States implied that this major sanction—the right of self-taxation—would not be available to Jewish communities in America. It was therefore necessary to develop new approaches to pursue these charitable and eleemosynary objectives, or else the objectives had to be sacrificed. The problem was further complicated because the intimate relations previously existing between religious and social objectives no longer obtained. Therefore, the orthodox community of Europe did not sharply differentiate expenses of providing the poor with basic education from providing them with minimal food, clothing, and shelter. Likewise, the support of communal officials

whose primary duty was the supervision of ritual slaughter was on the same level of urgency as the maintenance of a communal burying ground. The religious, educational, and social objectives of the community were of one piece. The decline of orthodoxy implied that the important religious sanctions which gave cohesion to older Jewries were no longer operative. Thus, if American Jews were to continue to take care of their sick and needy, they had to surmount the difficulties brought about through the loss of religious cohesion as well as the loss of the power of self-taxation.

4. Religious and educational organizations were hard-pressed in securing financial support from members of a community who no longer had to submit to compulsory taxation. But charitable enterprises such as hospitals, relief organizations and burial societies— enterprises that were social rather than educational or religious —were liberally supported. It was inevitable that they would be. Irrespective of the break with orthodoxy, most American Jews did not desire to sever all their contacts with Judaism. Some did, but the majority did not. Despite their much weakened interest in matters religious and cultural, they were able to give expression to their Jewishness by continuing to support fellow Jews who were in need of assistance. Here was one tie with the past which did not depend on ideology. Thus the support of charitable undertakings became a focus for community efforts at a time when common religious objectives were no longer present. Charity was neutral ground on which many different groups could meet without precipitating a host of ideological conflicts.

5. The leadership of organized Jewish charities in the United States was naturally assumed by the older and wealthier families, first those of Spanish and later those of German extraction. Their work had a large component of noblesse oblige. Throughout the latter half of the nineteenth and the early part of this century the direction and management of Jewish charitable enterprises was controlled principally by a relatively small group of conscientious Jews largely of German extraction. Moreover, since this group con-

tributed most of the funds that were raised, it was not surprising that they exercised control. The fact that the raising of charitable funds as well as the management of charitable institutions is by definition a "leisure-time" activity (except for employees), class distinctions usually operative in social relations persisted in this arena. Wealthy Jews of German extraction founded most of the charitable enterprises, gave most of the money for their continuing support, and played the principal part in controlling their destinies.

6. This emphasis on the important role of the older families should not obscure the fact that the newer immigrants, primarily from Eastern Europe, almost from the day of their arrival, also participated in communal enterprises. There were the Landsmann-schaften and the lodges—organizations created to enable the new immigrants to aid their less fortunate brethren both in this country and in Europe. The absence of any general communal support for religious and educational institutions forced those immigrant groups who retained an interest in traditional values to provide the financial means to support their synagogues and their schools.

7. Charitable activities became a major focus of Jewish communal effort. The fact that many Jews had at best only a slight interest in problems religious and educational led them to channel their energies into charitable activities. Since established Jewish families, like their Christian counterparts, usually did not take an active part in politics, charitable undertakings became one of the few appropriate areas where a communal-minded individual could spend himself.

8. From the point of view of the wealthy, charitable activities had much to recommend them. The community was sufficiently fluid, and the need for assistance sufficiently great, so that it was a relatively easy matter for any person of means to secure for himself through liberal donations a position of communal prominence. Since there was no formal organization of the community new agencies could easily be established if the funds were forthcoming. There were no effective social controls. This was the era of free

competition in charitable agencies. There was always a place at the top for the person who was willing to foot the bill. There were no standards other than financial ability and integrity.

9. A pattern of raising and spending funds for charitable purposes was established which had several significant implications, not only for that day but for the future:

A. Charity became the almost exclusive prerogative of the wealthy. It was they who contributed the funds; who set the policy; who hired the staff; who frequently even selected the beneficiaries.

B. Particular programs were supported if they caught the interest of a sponsor; otherwise they were stillborn. The only priorities that were evolved were in the field of general relief. But even within this broad area, there was no mechanism to distinguish the more essential from the less essential.

C. It is likely that a man who donates a large sum will exercise a considerable influence on how the money should be expended. But significant differences can be noted between the individual who sets up general policies to govern the expenditure of his gift and the person who takes over the active direction of its disbursement. Many men could not find other outlets for their surplus energies, and many women had a surplus of time; hence lay directors were exceedingly active in the day-to-day operations of the organizations to which they had contributed liberally.

D. Since there is no necessary correlation between a man's ability to make money and his capacity to spend it wisely; and more particularly since marriage to a wealthy man does not imply the acquisition of managerial skills, it was inevitable that the direction of many organizations was relatively inefficient.

E. The preoccupation of many donors with the day-to-day operations of "their" organizations placed the salaried personnel and volunteer staffs largely at the mercy of the whims of the major benefactors. This had particularly serious implications for the so-called "professional" staff whose security and advancement, and of course initial appointment, was primarily a function of an ability to "get along" with the wealthy.

10. It was inevitable that the day of free competition in charitable enterprises would come to an end. The marked inefficiency resulting from a complete lack of communal planning was certain to impress itself on the very wealthy who carried such a large part of the total burden. The intensity of the competition became even greater as some of the newer immigrants succeeded in business and sought outlets for their surplus funds and energies. Since the established leadership was composed almost exclusively of a group that was tightly knit in social and cultural background, it failed to make room for the newcomers. But an exclusionist policy could not succeed. Those who had money to spend soon found outlets. The duplication and overlapping became that much greater.

11. The growth and development of modern welfare funds and federations resulted only in part from a desire of the established leadership to increase the efficiency of operations in the respective charitable organizations; primarily they represented an effort to cut the excessive costs in time and money involved in raising the necessary funds for the support of a galaxy of institutions. Increased coordination and integration were sought in fund-raising, not in agency operations. Potential contributors felt themselves harassed by the inordinate number of separate appeals and the more thoughtful members of the community were increasingly sensitive to the high cost involved in securing charitable donations. Moreover, the expansion of charitable enterprises had proceeded at a pace which no longer made it possible for a limited few to assume sole, or even primary responsibility, for their support. Once larger numbers in the community had to be approached, the costs of campaigning became a significant consideration.

12. More recently, since the advent of Hitler and the accelerated upbuilding of Palestine, the total sums of money which American Jews were asked to provide, not only for support of their local and national institutions, but primarily for overseas needs, were so greatly increased that a tremendous effort had to be devoted to the task of money raising. Three groups carried most of the responsibility; lay leadership which continued to play a strategic role; the professionals who had slowly secured a place in the administration of various charitable enterprises, where they were no longer directly dependent on the whims and fancies of individual benefactors; and the new specialists, the experts in money raising. These groups were confronted with the tremendously difficult problem of devising means of raising very sizeable sums from a voluntary community in which the leadership had no legal sanction to extract contributions from those able to make them. Although these experts developed a wide range of techniques, their major reliance, especially in the large urban centers was based on the effective organization of trades, especially those which boasted considerable numbers of wealthy Jews. The logic of this approach was predicated upon the belief that the financial position of a potential contributor could be most correctly appraised by his business associates. By drafting a leader in the trade to act as chairman, it was possible to apply a combination of business and social pressures.

13. Fund raising has reached an exceptionally high level of efficiency. The Jews contribute considerably more per capita than any comparable group in the United States. Moreover, they have demonstrated a willingness to keep their contributions at a high level year after year. There are, however, various aspects of the problem that give cause for concern:

A. Despite the rather effective organization which has been developed in most communities to facilitate raising money for Jewish purposes, a tremendous effort is still being devoted to fund raising per se. This is true not only when measured in terms of the time and effort of the lay leadership and their assistants; it is reenforced when account is taken of the number of paid workers and the other sizeable expenses of campaigning. This cost in personnel and money looms very large in view of the fact that it represents not a one-time but an annual expenditure. Although during the last decade there was little change in the objectives for which the funds were to be used, the same intense efforts have been put forward year after year. Although the mechanisms for extracting contributions are, when measured in terms of results, highly efficient, they possess little "carry-over" value from one year to the next.

B. The time and effort required of the leadership to establish and carry through a successful campaign have been so great as to preempt almost its entire energies. This has had serious consequences. A leadership grows from exposure and experience. Engulfed in fund raising, it was inevitable that Jewish leadership would remain to a large degree intellectually sterile. This overconcentration has resulted in the leadership's playing a minor role in planning and guiding the enterprises which are the beneficiaries of the campaigns. The pattern has been altered radically. Several decades ago, the typical benefactor meddled so frequently and so inexpertly in the daily operations of his "pet" organization that it was impossible for the professional personnel to perform efficiently and effectively. Now the boards of directors do not exercise even that minimum of general supervision required to insure that the administrative group is carrying out established policies. There is too little reappraisal of basic objectives and established working procedures—clearly the responsibility of the lay leadership. The more intelligent leaders are distressed that they are on a treadmill and that their sole activity is raising money. Yet they see no escape from their dilemma. Now that the most acute phase of the overseas emergency has passed, perhaps a long-overdue correction will begin to take place.

14. For some time forces have been operating which may reduce the gap between the time devoted to fund-raising and the time devoted to organizational planning and management. The initial success of the leaders in organizing Jews into a loosely structured community was largely a result of efforts devoted to charity because this was the only area which was free of ideological conflict. But these initial efforts to establish welfare funds and federations soon disclosed that it was not possible to restrict the new organizations to problems connected with the collection of funds. Relatively early in the development of these welfare funds it became clear that there was a close relationship—an inevitable one—between unified efforts at fund-raising and unified control over allocations. It was the latter—control over allocations—that precipitated anew conflicts of value. The sums required by the participating organizations —local, national, and overseas—usually exceeded by a considerable margin the amounts that the community could raise. Since the budget of each beneficiary could not be met in full, it was necessary to develop criteria to guide the allocations. For many years, key decisions about allocations have been subject to negotiations on a national level between the major organizations responsible for overseas services. There was basic agreement among American Jews that the bulk of the funds should be spent abroad, but the distribution between European relief and Palestinian reconstruction was an area of contention. There has been repeated evidence during the past years that the officials of the contesting organizations were influenced by "grass roots" sentiments in favor of joint fund-raising.

15. A further consequence of the need to establish priorities has been that both the national agencies and local organizations have made available factual analyses of the programs and operations of the beneficiaries of the fund-raising efforts. These studies have been largely of indifferent quality; worse still, the leadership and the membership has had little experience in using data for evaluating programs and performance.

16. It is not surprising, but it is regrettable that the principal organizations which in the past made available only a minimum of

information concerning their programs and operations should look askance at the prospect of increasing the information which they make public. In part this reluctance reflects the disinclination of executives to operate in the full glare of publicity. In part it reflects a belief that badly needed resources should not be deflected from essential programs into research investigations. But the major reason back of this widespread disinclination of many established organizations to make their operating data available is the fear that their figures will be manipulated and interpreted by competing organizations which are seeking larger allocations. The leadership of many organizations has been accustomed to employ the techniques of "power politics" in furthering the interests which they represent. The emphasis on statistics and research is new and involves approaches which they can not easily control. But the trend is definitely in the direction of critical evaluation.

17. American Jews are becoming aware once again that the essence of a community is not reducible to an isolated activity, or to even a series of uncorrelated activities, but requires an integrated pattern which must be rooted in a scheme of basic values. The last five decades have seen these values so greatly in flux that no pattern was discernible. The overemphasis on charitable enterprises, at least an exclusive emphasis, reflected a particularly narrow value scheme. The value problem has begun to reemerge in the community's search for a reasonable basis on which to allocate the charitable funds which are raised. Charity can no longer be an end in itself; but it will take much intelligence and devotion before a more adequate basis for communal action is developed.

VI: ISRAEL

1. The ties between the United States and Israel are of long standing. As far back as colonial times, representatives of the Jewish community in Palestine came to this country to solicit alms. And as transportation improved, the number and frequency of these visitors increased. The fact that these representatives of Palestinian Jewry found it worthwhile to travel half around the world was proof that American Jews, like all other Jews in the Diaspora, felt a deep emotional attachment to the land of their fathers and were willing to express these ties through charitable contributions. However, it would be false to exaggerate the contacts which existed between America and Palestine during the seventeenth, eighteenth, and early nineteenth centuries. Apart from charitable contributions, the only manifestation of concern with this historic tie is found in the writings of Major Noah who, in the first decades of the nineteenth century, developed a plan for the resettlement of large numbers of Jews in Palestine.

2. Although several of the principal leaders of modern Zionism were German Jews, the movement, as the active and organized purchase of land in Palestine and the resettlement thereof by Jewish pioneers, had its origin in Eastern Europe. Some of the ideological spur came from the West, but the movement was definitely "Eastern" —Galician, Polish, Lithuanian and Russian. Modern industrialism had undermined the ghetto life of Eastern Jewry, and no place had been found for the Jews in the life of the Slavic peoples—partly because they did not want to share in it, and partly because they were not permitted to. The Czars would permit the Jews to play a role in the expansion of Russian nationalism only at the price of renouncing their Judaism, a price too high for the ghetto dwellers. Under pressure from within and without, many succeeded in escaping to the United States. But the still larger numbers who remained behind had to find some meaning and direction for their lives. Except for the diminishing group of the ultra-orthodox whose

orientation remained primarily internal—that is, they remained preoccupied with the historic values of Judaism—the masses had to find new positive values if they were not to sink into hopeless despair. Zionism became a major force in their re-orientation.

3. The large numbers who emigrated to the United States had shared the experiences of those who remained behind. Although it was inevitable that many of the newcomers' values would be altered under the impress of American conditions, their old experiences were never completely transformed or lost. The difficulties and the sufferings of Eastern Jewry were part and parcel of the life experience of the immigrants who therefore remained sympathetic to and interested in the efforts of those who remained behind. Thus, as Zionism assumed an increasingly important role in the communal life of Eastern Jewry, it was able to count upon a friendly reception from many Eastern Jews who had emigrated to the United States, South Africa, and other parts of the world. The Jews in the New World were so closely identified with those who remained behind that when Zionism, during its formative period failed to win universal support in Eastern Europe—both the extreme orthodox and the extreme left, which concentrated on economic reform as hope of salvation, remained negative—the resistances were also reflected in the United States where neither the extreme right nor the extreme left was sympathetic.

4. The growth of Zionism in the United States was affected not only by antagonistic minorities among the immigrant groups but it was also challenged and fought by the older group, particularly the Jews whose families had emigrated from Germany. This conflict was inevitable. At the turn of the century, Reform Judaism in the United States possessed a fighting ideology characterized by a denial of the major elements of Jewish tradition. The Reform movement, defining Judaism as a system of religious belief, not as a way of life, made a systematic attempt to free itself from the obligations of tradition. So negativistic an approach could find no sympathy for the affirmations implicit in Zionistic philosophy. It was inevitable that, without an intimate knowledge of conditions in Eastern

ISRAEL

Europe and therefore with little sympathy for the plight of the large masses of disenfranchised Jews, Reform Judaism would oppose Zionism. But this opposition cannot be explained solely by lack of knowledge and lack of sympathy. Zionism was aggressively Jewish; it was positive and constructive. From first to last, it was Jewish. Its insistence that there could be no solution for the Jewish problem except through the re-establishment of a normal environment for Jews, and then only in Palestine, was a constant challenge and taunt to Reform Judaism which, especially in the United States, had come dangerously close to promulgating a philosophy of total assimilation.

5. Shortly before the Balfour Declaration was issued and especially thereafter, cracks began to develop in the wall of opposition to Zionism erected in the United States by the older immigrants from Germany who were also the leaders of Reform Judaism. There were some leaders, especially lay leaders among the German-Reform group who had retained a rather broad sympathy for historic Jewish values and who therefore were able to appreciate the forces which were at work to strengthen Zionism among the Eastern masses. Moreover, this group, which was considerably more secure in its own Jewishness, did not feel challenged and exposed by the actions of other Jews, even though they did not necessarily approve of either their objectives or tactics.

6. With the establishment of the Mandate in 1922, the upbuilding of Palestine became for the first time a realistic enterprise. The number of Jewish settlers increased substantially and with them came a general quickening of the economic and cultural pulse. It is worth noting, however, that despite the fertile soil which Eastern Europe had long provided for Zionist ideals and ambitions, the opportunities provided by the Mandate were not fully utilized by Jews living in the Old World. The explanation for this is probably that the establishment of the Mandate coincided with the establishment of "democratic regimes" in Eastern Europe which replaced the absolutistic government of the Czars. Many Jews hoped that the world would in fact become "safe for democracy." The war in

which they suffered grievously was over and they were able to convince themselves that the future in their own lands would eventually be brighter. Palestine was far off and they concluded from what they heard and read that Palestine was not a land of milk and honey, but a land of malaria swamps and sand dunes.

7. The absence of a pronounced desire of the Jewish masses in Eastern Europe to emigrate to Palestine (those within the borders of Soviet Russia were not permitted to leave) was paralleled in the United States by a rather slow and halting growth in the Zionist movement. The movement did gain some impetus from the establishment of the Mandate; more money was raised than previously. But, by any objective test, the resources of American Jewry were scarcely tapped. Since American Zionists had never indicated that they, their wives, and their children would one day emigrate to Palestine, it was exceedingly difficult for them to mobilize mass support in the United States. Had European Jewry asked for help, then help would probably have been forthcoming from the United States. But in the absence of any major interest on the part of the Jewish masses to emigrate, it was inevitable that the American scene would reflect what it did—a continuing interest and sympathy for the work of the pioneers, at least among that group of Americans who had been brought within the orbit of Zionistic activity. In terms of numbers and effort, one of the most significant groups were the women who, even prior to World War I had organized themselves into Hadassah and had selected as their primary mission the support of health and child services in Palestine.

8. The establishment of the Mandate also elicited support from the non-Zionist groups. Several of their leaders had a genuine interest in the growth of Palestine; they had participated in the Peace Conference and later had directed substantial efforts toward providing capital for the new country and toward the support of such non-political activities as the Hebrew University. Just prior to the accession of Hitler to power, which radically altered the entire setting, a plan had been worked out for the non-Zionist leadership to co-operate formally in the upbuilding of Palestine. Reference to

this fact has more significance as a measure of intent than of accomplishment, however, for after the plan of the expanded Jewish Agency was finally evolved, it failed to accomplish its principal purpose of enhancing the support received from the non-Zionistic groups. Sudden changes in leadership and the onset of the Great Depression radically altered the environment in which cooperation was to proceed.

9. The steps leading up to the creation of the Jewish Agency were indicative of the changing attitudes of the non-Zionists who were slowly admitting the possibility that the movement was tenable, even if they were not ready for a warm espousal of the cause. As the Jewish pioneers in Palestine gave evidence of increasing accomplishments, it was no longer defensible for any critic to maintain that the effort was completely invalid. Others were making the efforts and the results were beginning to speak for themselves. The point of difference that remained between Zionist enthusiasts and other members of the community related rather to the relative emphasis which each group placed on economic expansion, as against the political objectives of the movement.

10. The rapid deterioration in the position of European Jewry following the advent of Hitler to power, and the consequent desire and need of large numbers of European Jews to emigrate basically altered the role of Palestine in Jewish affairs. Except for the United States, emigrants could go only to Palestine. Whatever his rationale, it became increasingly difficult for any American Jew to maintain a negative attitude toward Jewish expansion in Palestine. The numbers who could be admitted into the United States were definitely limited, not only by law but by administrative encumbrances. Moreover, the early and middle thirties witnessed a major economic depression and the more cautious leaders of American Jewry were fearful that too large and too indiscriminate an immigration might give impetus to the latent anti-Semitism in this country. Desirous of helping Jews escape from the Hitler menace, but fearful of creating a new menace in the United States, a considerable number of the dominant leaders looked with favor upon Palestine as an

alternative haven. They were willing to put aside their ideological misgivings and reappraise the Palestine problem in terms of refugees and rehabilitation.

11.   During the late thirties, when the mandatory power placed increasing obstacles in the path of Jewish expansion in Palestine, culminating in the White Paper of 1939, most American Jews were sufficiently resentful to oppose actively British policy. Although the vast majority of American Jews did not suddenly become politically active, they felt themselves increasingly obligated to help their brethren in distress. They realized the need to close their ranks in order to offer effective opposition. One evidence of this trend was the establishment of the United Jewish Appeal which became a common ground for both Zionists and non-Zionists. The deep-seated differences between the two groups were not obliterated by the establishment of a unified organization for fund-raising purposes; they were simply brought under control sufficiently to permit joint action. Further proof that deep-seated ideological conflicts were giving way under the pressure of a menacing international situation can be found in the sizeable increases in the funds contributed by American Jews for overseas relief and Palestinian development.

12.   The outbreak of World War II turned the menace into a reality. The early German victories soon placed in jeopardy the lives of all European Jews other than those living in England and in Soviet Russia. For a considerable time Rommel's successes in North Africa held the threat of annihilation over Palestinian Jewry. Not since the time of the Crusades had the fortunes of Jews in the several parts of the world sunk so low. The only exceptions were the American Jews who, relatively speaking, were politically safe and economically secure. Conscious of the kindly way in which fate had treated them and sensitive to the plight of their brethren overseas, American Jews made strenuous efforts to assist those so sorely in need of help. The extent to which they could actually help was necessarily limited, but they intensified their efforts and raised ever larger funds for relief.

13. Even while the war was raging, a few were looking forward to the end of the fighting and the beginning of the reconstruction. Palestinian Jewry, which for a considerable time had been so close to the battlefront, became increasingly aware that the war would result in great changes in established international relations, especially between the major European powers and their African and Asian colonies and satellites. And Palestinian Jewry made plans for such opportunities as history might offer. Its leaders announced that with the coming of peace Palestinian Jews would seek political freedom through the establishment of a Jewish State. When the leadership thus openly declared their intention about ultimate political objectives for the first time since the ambiguous wording of the Balfour Declaration had enforced upon them a policy of caution and evasion, they anticipated the support of a large segment if not the overwhelming majority of American Jews. And their estimate was proved correct. Although many circumstances surrounding the establishment of the State could not have been foreseen and must be accounted fortuitous, the calculation of the Palestinian leadership that they could count on American Jewry for active support proved to be sound planning.

14. American Jews were, at most, a force of secondary importance in the establishment of the political platform of Palestinian Jewry. The leadership in this country was, however, so aggressive that its determination and optimism undoubtedly contributed to the crystallization of Palestinian opinion; American Zionists encouraged the Palestinian leaders to increase their demands and to shorten the deadline for their realization. They could offer advice and encouragement, and at times might even advocate caution and restraint because of possible reactions on American public opinion and policy, but in the last analysis Palestinian Jewry was responsible for working out its own fate. It is by no means certain that the dominant leaders in American Zionism were fully aware that this was so, but nevertheless they supported a policy that gave comfort and assistance to the Palestinian leaders.

15. American Zionists had been able to make two major contributions to the establishment of Israel. First, by fully exploiting the advantages inherent in the United Jewish Appeal, they were able to raise very large sums of money for Palestine. The United Jewish Appeal made it possible to procure funds—very sizeable funds—from members in the community who might not have contributed at all had they been solicited solely on behalf of Palestine. Secondly, they succeeded in mobilizing public opinion and, thereby, influencing, to a considerable degree, American foreign policy in the Near East. However, despite periodic deviations, American foreign policy has been consistently friendly to the Jews in Palestine. This is not surprising since there are only two reasons which might have caused the United States to follow an anti-Zionist policy. If it had been convinced that Great Britain would be able to work out a sensible solution, in the normal course of events the United States would have supported British efforts. In fact, for a long time it did support Britain until it became obvious that even with American help, Great Britain would never be able to work out a compromise solution. The second reason was oil. The Near Eastern output and reserves are important, very important, and as long as it appeared that American support of Palestinian Jewry would jeopardize its preferred position with respect to Arabian oil, American policy-makers had every reason to proceed cautiously. But once it became clear that Arab threats were one thing and Arab actions another, the United States realized that its support of Palestinian Jewry would not jeopardize its interest in Arabian oil. American Zionists have good reason to feel proud of the contribution which they made to the creation of Israel. But the fact that the State exists is, in the first instance, a testimonial to the integrity and devotion of Palestinian Jews to an ideal; secondarily, it is evidence of the inflexibility and gross errors of recent British policy.

16. The relations of American Jews to Palestinian Jewry when the State of Israel was established can be summarized as follows:

A. The overwhelming majority of American Jews felt a personal pride in the accomplishments of the Israelis. There was a universal exaltation because the major objective of a State had finally been reached despite the almost insuperable hurdles to its achievement. For the first time an objective which had at the onset appeared as an illusion and which later bore all the earmarks of a gamble, took firm shape.

B. After the outbreak of World War II an increasing number of American Jews participated actively in undertakings which were directly or indirectly aimed at the creation of a Jewish State in the Near East. For the most part their participation was limited to financial contributions; but many did more— in the field of public relations, on the political front, and by aiding the Jews to defend themselves through technical and other types of assistance.

C. Although the number of rabid anti-Zionists had been diminishing for a long time, it was Jewish determination and, finally, Jewish military prowess which succeeded in winning the admiration of almost all American Jews. There was no longer one group of Zionists and another of anti-Zionists; there were the extremely active Zionists and the more passive group.

17. The many successful efforts which American Zionists had made during the war and immediately thereafter to mobilize world opinion in favor of a Jewish Palestine reflected the strength and force of the organized movement in the United States. The movement was large and it had developed great momentum. Once the State was established, the organization lost its major objective. This was more or less inevitable. During the struggle the protagonists could not divert any part of their energies to planning for the period after victory. The establishment of Israel has had the following impact upon American Zionism:

A. The organizations whose major mission was public relations are left in mid-air. Their major objective has been achieved. They cannot become operating units of the new State unless their key personnel are willing to renounce their American citizenship. This presents an insuperable obstacle because these organizations are composed of Americans who intend to remain Americans.

B. The important fund-raising organizations were also affected by the creation of the new State. One reason why the leadership of the American Zionist movement was so powerful is the control which it exercised over so large a part of the charitable contributions. It was inevitable that the leadership, estopped from political activity, would redouble its efforts to maintain its influence through controlling the fund-raising mechanism. The fact that American tax legislation and general American policy discourages American citizens from making direct contributions to foreign governments seemed to stimulate the efforts of the established Zionist leadership to exercise strategic control over charitable funds. But the logic of events was against them; it was simply a question of time before they lost their monopolistic control. Short of funds, and short of foreign exchange, it was absolutely essential for the new State of Israel to exercise strategic controls over the expenditure of all foreign exchange, including American contributions. The fact that the American Zionist leadership was committed to a general ideological position which had no real strength within Israel made it that much more important for the new State to exercise general direction over the expenditure of these crucial funds.

18. It was inevitable that so fundamental an event as the establishment of the new State of Israel would precipitate a host of problems for American Jews which could be resolved only slowly.

A. Although it may appear that the established Zionist organizations in the United States no longer have a *raison d' etre,* it is obvious that they represent a type of communal asset which should continue to be effectively utilized, for as long as possible. Clearly, for a considerable number of years the new State will be greatly dependent for its growth and development on a friendly American foreign policy. Although it would be obviously improper for an organization of American Jews to seek to influence directly the formation of American foreign policy with respect to Israel, it would likewise be unwise to disband all Zionist organizations which can still make a contribution, especially in public relations.

B. Similarly on the charitable front: very large sums had been collected and sent to Palestine for many years and since the new State doubtless will require additional large sums for many years to come, there are serious dangers inherent in disbanding the established fund-raising organizations. On the other hand, there is an urgent need to shift the emphasis from charity to investment capital. If Israel is to absorb two hundred and fifty thousand immigrants per year for three or four years, the financing of such a colossal undertaking cannot possibly be insured solely by charitable contributions. New approaches will be required to insure the flow of sizeable capital funds from the United States to Israel different in kind and degree from those which have proved effective in raising charitable contributions. Hence, one must look forward to major changes in the established organizational pattern.

C. Current efforts to deal with the problems precipitated by the establishment of the new State by finding new objectives for the old organizations are predicated on the logic of conserving so far as possible the structures and values of established organizations. But this approach reflects to a large degree the absence of sound alternatives. Current floundering emphasizes the fact that the general cultural implications of Zionism had never been meaningfully integrated into the fabric of American Judaism. As long as the problem was limited to raising money and propagandizing, American Zionists clearly saw their task. But the time is soon approaching, if it is not already here, when American Jews must begin to deal with much more complicated issues, namely their true responsibilities to the State of Israel, and, in turn, the contributions which they hope the new State will make to their culture in this country.

19. For a long time to come American Jews will undoubtedly play a large part in the expansion of Israel, because Israel cannot expand without foreign capital, specialized skills, and expert personnel. And it is to American Jewry that Israel must look for primary assistance. But the basic relations between American Jews and the Jews in Israel will not be delimited to these economic considerations. There are at least three major foci that are relevant:

A. The development of Judaism in the United States from this time on will be materially influenced by developments in Israel. Despite the fact that heretofore Zionist activity in America has been largely limited to economic and political considerations, it is both essential and desirable that henceforth the religious and the cultural bonds be accentuated. Much of the current turmoil and confusion in Zionist affairs reflects the absence of adequate religious and cultural bonds.

B. The very fact that Israel will expand and develop and will attract to it many Jews who are now living precariously throughout the world—this inevitable centripetal force which Israel will exert, makes it particularly necessary for American Jews to consider the welfare of scattered minorities who will continue to live outside of Palestine. Israel will be able to make a contribution to them because Israel will make a contribution to the whole of the Diaspora, but it will be a cultural contribution. The obligation to provide material assistance to these scattered minorities becomes a heightened responsibility of American Jews.

C. The problem of double allegiance which is still bruited about can be dismissed as symptomatic of insecure and confused thinking. But there are several problems, nevertheless, growing out of the establishment of Israel, which

face American Jews in their relations to other Americans.
Many Americans must be curious as to whether their Jewish
friends and neighbors entertain the idea of emigrating to
Israel now or in the future. Israel cannot long escape the
pressures inherent in the struggles between the East and
West. It is clear that Israel will do what it can to remain
neutral. It may be forced on occasion to follow a policy
different from that of the United States. No one can foresee
how different this policy may be. When that happens, questions will again be raised about the relation of American
Jews to the Israelis. But the answers to these particular
questions will be found in the more general answers of
how American Jews work out their basic relations to the
Gentile community.

VII: THE GENTILE WORLD

1. The answer to the problem of Jewish survival, if one defines survival as a problem, lies in the explanation of how this small ethnic group, conscious of its own fate, has been able to keep itself alive in a hostile world. An extremist would explain Jewish survival in terms of the willingness of the hostile majority to place some restraint on its negativism toward the Jews, for clearly if it were solely a matter of military strength, the majority long ago could have successfully liquidated the last remnants of the Chosen People.

2. In a certain sense, the Gentiles were "ambivalent"; periodically, when emotions got out of control, they set out to slaughter the Jews, but their hatred was never so pronounced or so sustained that they were able to finish the job. As a matter of fact, it is questionable whether the Church, once it became well-established, really wanted to see the Jews disappear completely. In addition to the moral issue, which made it difficult for the leaders of the Church to sanction and support pogroms, there is much evidence to suggest that the Church found it desirable to preserve a remnant of Israel, largely as an historic testimony to the truth of Christianity.

3. Aside from special interests of the authorities in their welfare, the survival of the Jews must in considerable part be ascribed to the safety of dispersal. Although there were heavy concentrations of Jews in Europe—in Spain, in the Rhineland, later in Lithuania, Poland, and the Balkans—they were never within the domain of a single secular or even a single ecclesiastical power. Therefore, when their fortunes deteriorated in one country or in one group of countries, there were Jews in other places who were temporarily free from intensified harassment. Thus, the very weakness of Diaspora Jewry was in fact one of its strengths.

4. History records no other people who were able to absorb major defeats at the hands of their enemies such as the Jews suffered

when they were conquered by the Assyrians, the Babylonians, the Syrians, the Romans; who were able to emerge from the trials and tribulations of the Crusades, the Expulsion from Spain, the major and minor pogroms under the Czars, who finally were even able to start anew after Hitler had almost succeeded in wiping them from the face of Europe. Impressive as this record is, it is well to remember that the Jews paid a colossal price for survival. But the fact that they did survive is perhaps more important than the price they paid. This much is certain: only a people who had developed a great aptitude for living among adversaries and for escaping from the control of aggressors could have established such a record. There must be imbedded deep in the collective experience of the Jews a philosophy and a stratagem—in fact, multiple stratagems— for surviving amidst hostile majorities. The Jews had no option about their relations to the Gentile world. It was not an intellectual problem with which they could concern themselves or, if they preferred, could ignore. They had to concern themselves, all of the time, because their very lives depended upon working out tolerable, if not satisfactory, solutions. But survival was never an end in itself, only a means to the preservation of Judaism's distinctive values.

5. From the beginning of the Diaspora, the basic approach of Jewry to the Gentile world has encompassed the following:

A. A safeguarding of the values of Judaism, to whose basic values the life of every member of the community was dedicated, and which could not be sacrificed even to protect the individual's life.

B. A realization that within these limits, there were actions which the Jewish community might take which could affect positively or adversely the immediate or future behavior of the Gentile majority.

C. A recognition that Jews as Jews could do little, if anything, to influence and modify the basic hostility of Christianity toward the tenets of Judaism.

6. Reformulated, these approaches have the following implications:

A. The constructive efforts of Diaspora Jewry revolved around certain values, including basic religious beliefs, which were important to all Jews. The long list of martyrs is proof that these values were held supreme. Admittedly, the average man is not born to die a martyr, and more Jews were converted to Christianity than died at the stake. But thousands upon thousands did die at the stake rather than forswear the faith of their fathers.

B. The Jews soon learned that despite periodic paroxysms of religious fervor, neither the Christian masses nor the Christian leadership considered the persecution of Jews a religious or civic duty. Thus the Jews were able to work out more or less successful arrangements with both the secular and the ecclesiastical authorities who for a sizeable price were willing to offer protection to Jewish life and property. This protection was withdrawn at the convenience of the authorities or when the masses were motivated to translate into action the intense prejudices that had been instilled into them.

C. The fickleness of their friends and the uncertainty of their security and protection were ample proof to all Jews that the favor of the Gentiles was shallow; that Christianity had a deep and uncompromising feud with Judaism; and that, except at the price of apostasy, the Jew could not mitigate this basic attitude in any fundamental respect. Realizing that he was hated and despised because he was a Jew, and turning his back on apostasy, the Jew realized that he would have to carry this burden all his days. As in the case of dispersion, so also in the case of personal vulnerability, a major liability became an asset because the Jew was compelled to turn his energies inward and live by, and for, his own values.

7. After repeated experiences which proved that even friendly neighbors could not always be relied upon when the floodgates of religious frenzy broke open, the Jews reconciled themselves to the lack of escape; and realized that they would always remain the direct or indirect target of the hostile Gentiles among whom they lived. So they, figuratively and literally, turned their backs on the peoples and cultures surrounding them and turned with heightened intensity to their own institutions and their own ways of life. In the extreme manifestation of this self-imposed isolation, such as expressed by Lithuanian Jewry of the nineteenth century, the Jews lived a more intense and complete Jewish life than had their forefathers in the Land of Israel who had had perhaps greater contact with the Gentiles than did the ghetto communities of the recent past.

8. There were, however, important Jewish communities in various parts of Europe which for varying lengths of time lived in close association with their Gentile surroundings. This was true of the important Jewish communities on the Iberian Peninsula where the Jews had an organic relationship with Spanish culture, first Moorish and then Christian; where the Jewish masses lived and worked as did the Spanish masses; and where the Jewish elite shared with the Spanish elite the important positions in commerce, science, and statecraft. And there were periods in Italian and Dutch history when the same intimate relation existed between the Jewish minority and the Gentile majority. But these important examples should be viewed more as exceptions than the rule. For the most part the large Jewish communities of the Rhineland and the Palatinate and later the still larger communities of Poland and Russia represented the "isolated" rather than the "integrated" type of Jewish community.

9. The nineteenth century brought with it a series of changes so fundamental in character that many Jews and even some Gentiles believed that the lessons of history, the lessons of almost two millenia of relationship between Jew and Gentile, no longer had relevance. Three major developments took place, each of which had a significant bearing on this relationship:

A. The religious foundations of Christianity, hence of European life and culture, were seriously shaken first by the attack on the supernatural origins of the Bible and later, more generally, by the impact of the naturalistic (evolutionary) doctrine.

B. The Napoleonic wars and the simultaneous export of French doctrine gave marked impetus to the development of national states. The growth of secular power established a new set of values to which all individuals within the geographic confines of the state had to pledge support irrespective of their origins or their beliefs.

C. Coincident with the attack on formal religion and the impetus to the creation of national states was the spread of democratic ideas and ideals which propounded the theory of the innate value of the individual whose worth to society was to be measured not in terms of his ancestry or his "personal beliefs", but by his work for and affirmation of the ideals of an individualistic society.

10. Although the nineteenth century witnessed major structural changes in Western Europe, which were to exercise a pronounced influence on the relations between Jews and Gentiles, the development in the United States was truly unique; no comparable environment could be found in the pages of history. Of specific note in the American culture were the following:

A. Since the North American continent had never known feudalism, and since the Church had never become entrenched (although the Puritan ecclesiastics exercised great power in their communities), the secular power was not obliged to engage upon a struggle in order to establish its supremacy.

B. Where such struggles had taken place, as in Western Europe, the state was never completely successful. The entrenched groups retained residues of control, often including the privileges which were part and parcel of their heritage. In the United States, neither the Federal Constitution nor the

State Constitutions provided any special status for any
church. The separation between church and state in the
United States was, if not absolute, nevertheless substantial.

C. But perhaps the most important factor in the American
scene was the environment which was so conducive to a
deepening and strengthening of democracy. Although the
American development of democracy had a European coun-
terpart, its essential nature was strikingly different. Of
course there were classes in the United States; but the membership in each of the several classes was exceptionally fluid.
Through his own efforts, any man could gain entrance to a
new class; in turn, any individual who failed to prove his
worth might well be forced to sacrifice the class advantages
which were his at birth.

11. Historical changes of such magnitude could not take place
in the Gentile world without having a major influence upon the
Jews who lived within that environment. Along with the Gentiles,
the Jews of Western Europe and of the United States were greatly
affected, and before long, many of the Jews, if not all of them,
took a very positive attitude with respect to the new forces which
were developing in the world about them:

A. The attack on religion, especially on the supernatural foundations of Christianity, was not restricted to Christianity
itself. The Hebraic tradition, with its emphasis on the Torah
as the word of God, likewise came under major attack by
the critics of supernaturalism. And as the attack gained
strength among the Jews themselves, it brought about a
major split in the religious structure and practices of the
Jewish communities in Western Europe and the United
States. The emancipated, convinced that the Pentateuch was
merely folklore, saw fit to divest themselves of the burden
of the law and of responsibility of conforming to traditional
practices. In short, they became reformed. And in the
place of disciplined orthodoxy, they substituted a rather

innocuous brand of ethical monotheism. By these actions, the Reform group expected that the gap between the orthodox Jew and the orthodox Christian, previously unbridgeable, would all but disappear, at least between Reform Judaism and liberal Protestantism.

B. The desire of the secular state to gain the loyalty and respect of all who lived within its borders was met by the desire of many Jews, who for so long had been politically disenfranchised, to participate fully and actively in the life of the state. Many Jews believed that the new forms created by the new state would abolish many of the old obstacles to their effective participation in the life of the communities and that therefore they as Jews could not fail to profit from this intensification of nationalism.

C. The uneven but nevertheless certain growth of democracy on both sides of the Atlantic was also viewed by the majority of Jews as a favorable omen for their own development. For the essence of democracy stresses that every individual is to be evaluated on his own merit, not by that of his parents or church. In every country, therefore, considerable numbers of Jews became ardent devotees of the democratic cause.

12. These developments in which so many Jews participated—developments which greatly weakened the orthodox foundations of Jewish belief and practice; which led many Jews to look to the national state for emancipation; which convinced other Jews that their future was bound up with the fate of democracy—had a major effect upon the vitals of Diaspora Jewry. For almost two thousand years the Jews had lived in a Christian world without concerning themselves greatly with the workings of that world. Their major preoccupation had been with the means and measures available to them to gain and keep a modicum of security. The nineteenth century saw large segments of Western European and American Jewry shift their orientation. For increasing numbers of Jews no longer sought and found their principal values in their own tradition but in the tradition and culture of the people among whom they

lived. A simple arithmetic relation was established: with every increase in interest and identity with the values of the West came a diminution in the respect for and adherence to their values of old. Of course, for some—a minority—the absorption of the new values led not to a proportionate discarding of the old, but to an attempted synthesis of the new and the old.

13. During the many centuries when Jewish communities found their anchorage in the shared experiences of old and in their common aspirations for the future, there was a sense of direction and meaning to Jewish existence, difficult and dangerous as that existence frequently was. It is questionable whether the manifold implications of exchanging this "inner" security and sense of direction for the apparently enhanced security and opportunity of the outside world were truly appreciated. But it was not very long before some of the wiser heads among the emancipated Jews realized that the exchange would lead to utter bankruptcy unless the promises of the Christian world were fulfilled in fact. To the extent that the weakened Church remained a dominant power; to the extent that the national state discriminated among those living within its borders; to the extent that democracy failed to make significant inroads into deeply ingrained class prejudice and discrimination—in short, to the extent that the developments, which at the beginning of the century appeared so propitious, failed to materialize or materialized only in part, the Jews would be in a precarious position. They had traded one kind of security for the hope, but not for the actuality, of another.

14. As far as the American scene is concerned, the following factors should be noted:

A. The large stream of immigrants of all nationalities which flowed from Europe into the United States for many decades eased the adjustment of the Jewish immigrants. In the long centuries of Jewish migration this was the first and only time when accretions of large numbers of Jews to a settled population were associated with large-scale additions from other groups. This gave a considerable "protective coloring" to Jewish immigration into the United States. However, despite this favorable situation, the different types of immigrants were accepted in varying degrees by the native population. Second and third-generation Americans found it easier to look with favor on immigrants from the British Isles and Northern Europe than to accept those who came from Central and Eastern Europe—at least to accept them as quickly and as unreservedly. Eventually these implicit distinctions among potential immigrants were written into the law to the marked disadvantage of the Italians, the Slavs, and the Jews.

B. While no church, Protestant or Catholic, had special status in the United States, under either federal or state law, it did not follow that organized religion was not potent on the American scene. Although there was considerable variation in the power and prestige of various religious groups in different parts of the country, there were few sections where organized religion was without influence. And wherever religion remained a potent force the members of the community were inevitably indoctrinated with an "anti-Jewish" bias, a basic element in the Christian tradition. Only the extreme liberal wing of Protestantism, and occasionally not even this wing, sought to reinterpret its tradition to reduce this bias to a minimum.

C. Although the United States is an increasingly successful experiment in democracy, it is well to emphasize that our democracy is still subject to continuing experimentation. The adjustment of Jews to American life and culture was greatly aided by the underlying trend toward democratic expression and experience. But general adherence to democratic ideals alone did not succeed in breaking down existing barriers for the exploitation of, and discrimination against, minorities, nor did it prevent the erection of new barriers. The Jews were among the sub-groups in the community which were particularly vulnerable to one or another variety of discrimination, particularly in the social and economic spheres of life.

15. Although it would be difficult to prove, it is reasonable to postulate that the Jewish immigrants who came to the United States represented a high proportion of individuals who sought their personal salvation through adjustment in the Gentile world, particularly the new world of the United States. The Jews who were still primarily traditionally oriented, who looked to Jewish belief and practice for primary guidance and support, tended to remain in the ghetto communities of Europe under the protective influence of Jewish institutions which had dominated their lives and that of their fathers'. Only when the Gentile world made life around them completely intolerable through unbearable economic oppression or pogroms did they contemplate re-locating in what they considered the pagan environs of the New World.

16. About the turn of the century the second- and third-generation American Jews who had surmounted the initial difficulties of adjustment—language, education and occupation—in short, the leaders of the German-Jewish community, became increasingly concerned with the barriers in the Gentile environment which stood in the way of their maximizing their own adjustment. In the first instance, they were concerned with the disabilities under which the Jews in the United States continued to labor, disabilities which were both perennial and sporadic. They were further concerned with the legal status of Jews in European and other countries, particularly when the basic rights of these fellow Jews were placed in serious jeopardy. During the first decade of this century, concrete steps were taken to establish appropriate organizations to enable American Jews to protect their own rights and to help in securing at least minimum rights for Jews in other countries. In the United States, these initial organizational efforts were directed not so much to broadening existing rights as to insuring that any attempt of others to circumscribe these rights would be successfully countered and nullified. These organizations were largely "defensive."

17. These initial efforts at "organized defense" had scarcely been undertaken when the difficulties of reaching voluntary agreement about the scope and content of an appropriate defense program became apparent. Even these first efforts to establish one body that could speak authoritatively for American Jewry revealed the inherent difficulties of securing agreement, voluntary agreement, concerning the focus of action, the range of action, and the means to be followed to secure the desired ends. The working out of a "defense program" revealed that such an undertaking would succeed only to the extent that prior agreement about values could be attained.

18. The individual Jew's approach to the Gentile world is determined by his approach to Judaism. The extent to which a Jew feels it desirable to concern himself with Gentile opinion; the extent to which he seeks the approval of the Gentile majority—these are determined in the first instance by his own philosophy and attitude toward Judaism. It was logical that those who had divorced themselves from the traditions of historic Judaism and who sought their security in the Gentile world would place a high value upon external adjustment. Inevitably their plight would be serious if the prospect for which they forsook tradition—that of adjusting themselves successfully to the Gentile majority—should not materialize. Then, surely, they would be left without fundamental security. There was another section of the Jewish population to whom this conscious preoccupation with the Gentile world was less obvious and important. This group was much larger, but much less prominent in terms of social status and economic power. It consisted primarily of the more recent immigrants from Eastern Europe who were still in the throes of overcoming the initial obstacles to adjustment—those of language, education, and occupation. Although this group had left behind them many cultural institutions which it was neither practical nor desirable to transplant to the New World; and although from necessity or desire they had departed from many traditional practices, they were still "Jewishly-oriented." The bond between the world which they had left and the world to which they had come was still very close. These immi-

grants had known at first-hand the difficulties confronting the ghetto communities of Eastern Europe and they considered themselves obligated to assist in overcoming them. In light of these differences of background and orientation between the older group of immigrants who had become increasingly estranged from the essential institutions of Judaism, and these newer immigrants, it is not surprising that a modus operandi could not easily be worked out. The distance between them was early demonstrated by the precipitation of the "Palestine issue." Those who aimed to improve their adjustment to the Gentile majority in the United States had little understanding of, or sympathy for, the resettlement of Palestine as a spiritual and temporal haven for large sectors of Diaspora Jewry. The Polish and Russian immigrants—aside from the Socialists who looked to Marx rather than to Moses—had no understanding of the negativism of any Jew toward the restoration of the Holy Land. The essential feature of this fundamental difference was their basic approach to Judaism; the Palestine issue was more symptom than cause. There were other differences which reinforced the basic schism, such as the fact that the older group belonged to the social and economic elite, and were in control of most of the positions of leadership in the Jewish community.

19. Until World War I, there was little challenge to the leadership exercised by the German-Jewish community. Up to this point the leaders had concentrated their efforts on a selected number of issues, primarily in maintaining the right of American Jews to travel freely on an American passport in any part of the Czar's domains and efforts aimed at blocking discriminatory legislation affecting immigration. The tremendous dislocation of the Jewish population of Eastern Europe during World War I, and the transformation of the Palestine issue from theory to fact after the issuance of the Balfour Declaration, presaged the need for American Jews to formulate policy for the peace settlements which were to take place with the ending of the war. Almost unified action was secured for the period of the Peace Conference. But the divisive forces were still so strong that when the overwhelming need for joint action

was removed, it was no longer possible to present a common front
to the Gentile world. Although time had contributed to narrowing
the gap between the new and the older immigrants, the gap was
still sufficiently wide to make unified action exceedingly difficult.

20. The nineteen twenties were relatively quiet although the
leaders of the community were concerned with the anti-Semitic
Dearborn Independent, the sporadic successes of the Ku Klux
Klan, and the other direct and indirect attacks upon the Jewish
community. It was the ascendancy of Hitler in the early nineteen
thirties which put the problem of Jewish relations to the Gentile
world in an entirely new setting. Hitler was not in power very long
before an increasing number of American Jews realized that he
represented a threat of first magnitude to the Jews in Germany and
the surrounding countries, and that his actions would contribute
materially to a rise of anti-Semitism in all parts of the world, including the United States. It was inevitable that in response to so
serious a threat, American Jewry would seek to build defenses
against it. But the old difficulties re-emerged: it was almost impossible to secure agreement among the various established organizations as to how best to meet and contain the evil force. In part, the
difficulties were a reflection of deep ideological differences in their
approaches to the essential core and meaning of Judaism. But important as these ideological differences were, perhaps even more
important by this time were the special interests of various organizations, particularly of the key leaders, each of whom was loath to
underwrite joint action if that meant circumscribing his own freedom of action and thus his prestige and power.

21. The intensification of concern with "defense activities"
during the past two decades makes it desirable to contrast recent
developments with the historic approach of Jewish communities to
their Gentile neighbors. We must first note that at present there
is no way of securing common consent and agreement on policy.
Each group has freedom of action subject only to the veto of the
people who support it. In earlier centuries, when the Jews were
organized into a disciplined community, it would have been incon-

ceivable that so vulnerable an area as relations to the Gentiles could
be left to any individual or group of individuals who desired to deal
with the problem. But this is the case in America today. Secondly, in
former generations, "defense actions" would never have pre-empted
the center of the stage of Jewish life. They were important—on
occasion, very important—but their importance derived from the
fact that the Jews were determined to protect and nourish the hard
core of Judaism, and were concerned with their external relations
only to the extent their physical security was threatened. Today at
least among large numbers of American Jews, the "defense activities" have usurped a position of priority. This was more or less
inevitable since many of these Jews have lost all interest in positive
Jewish values; their entire adjustment is externally oriented.
Finally, we are confronted with the amazing belief among American Jews—and it is quite prevalent though it contradicts the inner
wisdom of Judaism—that the basic attitudes of the Gentiles toward
the Jews can be significantly altered, if only the right "techniques"
are discovered and employed.

22. The word "defense" has been used here to describe the
galaxy of actions in which various Jewish organizations now engage in their attempt to influence the attitudes and behavior of
Gentile Americans toward Jews. It might be helpful to distinguish
three major levels of this activity:

A. The first may be identified as the area of "specific rights"
which on occasion are jeopardized through the actions of an
individual or an organized group of anti-Semites. In a real
sense this is the classic area for the work of defense organizations. It is difficult to see how ideological factors could
influence the decision of Jewish groups to engage in such
activity. It is obviously desirable for individuals and groups
to take action to protect themselves when they are threatened with attack, especially unfair attack. The only disagreement which might arise—other than the simple struggle
for organizational power and leadership—would relate to

the specific techniques to be employed in any given situation. Some might prefer to use the glaring lights of publicity; others might prefer to work unobtrusively. Although a relationship may exist between tactics and basic attitudes, generally a struggle over tactics is really a disguised struggle for organizational power and prestige.

B. The last decade in particular has witnessed an intensification of Jewish communal effort toward an expansion of "general rights". Many leaders have become impressed with the fact that the basic security of American Jews is intimately bound up with the maximal development of American democracy; that only as the discriminatory and other anti-democratic aspects of American life are eliminated can the Jew feel completely secure and become well-adjusted. Hence Jews have expended very sizeable sums to aid in eliminating these negative aspects of contemporary life. There are at least two questions worth raising with regard to this particular approach: Is it desirable and, perhaps even more important, is it feasible, for a relatively small minority in the United States, such as the Jews, to devote a substantial amount of effort and resources to accelerate basic social and economic changes by propagandizing on their behalf? Secondly, is it effective for Jews to organize themselves into specifically Jewish groups to contribute to these ends, or would it be more desirable for Jews to seek these ends by actively participating in the established groups that exist in the form of political parties on a local, state, and national level?

C. Closely related to these efforts to work toward a more speedy fulfillment of the American democratic ideal are the efforts which Jewish organizations are making to affect the fundamental philosophical and religious attitudes of American Gentiles toward the Jewish minority. Basically, the question is not whether the effort is desirable but simply whether it is feasible in view of the alternative demands on Jewish communal resources and the difficulties inherent in the project under consideration.

23. One cannot read Jewish history and review the current efforts of the Jewish community to improve its relations with the Gentile world without being impressed with the following facts:

A. It is exceedingly dangerous for a Jewish community to become preoccupied with influencing the attitudes and behavior of the Gentile majority because there is no basis for believing that it is likely to succeed in this effort. Moreover, in spending its limited resources for these purposes, the community will inevitably have to neglect the support of other institutions and activities which would most probably yield much higher returns in meaningful values and in basic security.

B. Any techniques which are employed in a propagandistic or political environment cannot be fully disclosed without destroying their efficacy. However, it is exceptionally dangerous for a voluntary community to collect money in sizeable amounts and to permit its expenditure without making a full disclosure of the relevant facts. The invitation to irresponsible leadership and unimaginative bureaucracy is overwhelming.

C. There are not many parallels in Jewish history to current-day Jewish life in the United States. As Americans, we all have not only the right but the responsibility to be concerned with the future of our democracy. Because of their vulnerability as a minority, the Jews are likely to pay a very high price for the imperfections which remain in our democracy. But it would seem to be the better part of wisdom for Jews rather to cooperate directly with like-minded citizens who are concerned with improving the structure and functioning of American democracy, than to concentrate their efforts in sectarian organizations. It would scarcely be stretching the point to contend that a sectarian approach itself runs counter to the basic traditions of American democracy. Moreover, the Jews will be able to do a much better job in accomplishing their specifically Jewish goals if they are not forced to dissipate their limited resources over too broad a front. As Americans, we are concerned with democracy; as Jews, with Judaism. Although there must be a relation between Judaism and democracy in America, they should not be identified or equated. The true strength of democracy is its highly variegated and diversified culture which permits each subgroup to develop its maximum potentialities and thereby contribute to the whole.

VIII: AGENDA

The attempt was made in the foregoing chapters to present in summary form a discussion of the more important issues confronting American Jewry in the hope that such a presentation could be used as a point of departure for further discussion and analysis. It may help to convey the burden of the major argument if the gist of each chapter is re-formulated in the form of a thesis or question.

I. Is it true that the principal organizations in contemporary Jewish life do not provide sufficient opportunity for interested individuals to participate in assessing the broad problems facing American Jewry? If so, what constructive steps can be taken to overcome this deficiency? (Chapter I)

II. The outstanding characteristics of Jewish life in the United States is the bifurcation of the community between professional leaders (lay and rabbinic) and their followers, with both groups characterized by an amazing lack of knowledge of, and sensitivity for, the basic facets of Judaism. (Chapter II)

III. Is it true that, despite the diversity of groups and organizations in American Jewish life, there is, in fact, a core of values which the vast majority of American Jews hold in common? If so, how can these common values be used as foundation stones on which to build a stronger and richer group life? (Chapter III)

IV. If Judaism in America can be characterized by a weakness in its religious base, what is the import of this fact? Is the synagogue regaining some of its lost strength and what actions, if any, should be taken to widen its influence? It is generally recognized that Jewish education has been able to reach only a small part of the population, and that it has failed to make the most of its opportunities in those sectors which it has reached. What steps can be taken to broaden the scope and improve the quality of Jewish education? (Chapter IV)

V. Although charitable undertakings, local, national, and international, provided the first and most potent focus for the organization of the Jewish community of the United States, the raising of funds for eleemosynary purposes may have reached the point where it is stultifying the growth of the community. What can be done to reduce the tremendous investment of time and effort now required to secure the necessary funds; and how can a greater degree of social control be obtained so that priorities are established among competing objectives and a higher degree of efficiency is maintained in the attainment of these objectives? (Chapter V)

VI. It is increasingly clear that the establishment of the State of Israel has precipitated a host of important problems for American Jews. If the old relations between American Jews and Jews living in Palestine must be altered because of the creation of the State, what areas hold the greatest promise for creative relations between the two communities? (Chapter VI)

VII. It is clearly necessary for American Jews to be concerned about their adjustment to the Gentile majority, but the question should be asked whether current efforts devoted to this end are reasonable; whether this problem merits the amount of resources expended and whether the specific focus of these efforts is sensible. (Chapter VII)

If these questions have merit, and if the answers to these questions are not self-evident, then certainly they should become the subject for investigation. For only as they are explored and only as agreement can be reached concerning the validity of the answers, can we look forward to the intelligent formulation of policy. The twentieth century is replete with terrifying evidence of people who have followed their hearts without reference to their heads. No people can afford a luxury, least of all the Jews whom history knows as the People of the Book.

BIBLIOGRAPHY

In order to keep the text compact, no statistical or other documentation has been included. It may be helpful, however, to list a few references which bear at least on segments of the foregoing analysis, if not on the entire presentation. With ready accessibility as the objective, references have been limited to books which are in print or which were widely distributed before going out of print.

American Jewish Yearbook, Vol. 50, 1948-49, Jewish Publication Society, 1949.

Baron, Salo W., *The Jewish Community,* Vol. 1, Jewish Publication Society, 1942.

Finkelstein, Louis, *The Jews,* Vol. 1 and Vol. 2, Harper, 1949.

Friedlaender, Israel, *The Jews of Russia and Poland,* Putnam, 1915.

Ginzberg, Eli, *Report to American Jews on Overseas Relief, Palestine and Refugees in the U. S.,* Harper, 1942.

Ginzberg, Louis, *Students, Scholars and Saints,* Jewish Publication Society, Reprinted 1943.

Janowsky, Oscar, Editor, *The American Jew,* Harper, 1942.

Kaplan, Mordecai M., *The Future of the American Jew,* Macmillan, 1948.

Lestschinsky, Jacob, *Crisis, Catastrophe and Survival,* Institute of Jewish Affairs of the World Jewish Congress, 1948.

Margolis, M. and Marx, A., *A History of the Jewish People,* Jewish Publication Society, 1927.

Nathan, Robert R., *et al., Palestine: Problem and Promise,* Public Affairs Press, 1946.

Radin, Max, *The Jews Among the Greeks and Romans,* Jewish Publication Society, 1915.

Sartre, Jean-Paul, *Anti-Semite and Jew,* Schocken Books, 1948.

Schachner, Nathan, *The Price of Liberty,* American Jewish Committee, 1948.

Weizmann, Chaim, *Trial and Error,* Harper, 1949.